THE LYON'S DEN CONNECTED WORLD

*A Reader's guide to groups, characters, and other information to
The Lyon's Den Connected World*

Updated Edition 1

July 2023

ARE YOU SIGNED UP FOR DRAGONBLADE'S BLOG?

You'll get the latest news and information on exclusive giveaways, exclusive excerpts, coming releases, sales, free books, cover reveals and more.

Check out our complete list of authors, too!

No spam, no junk. That's a promise!

Sign Up Here

www.dragonbladepublishing.com

Dearest Reader;

Thank you for your support of a small press. At Dragonblade Publishing, we strive to bring you the highest quality Historical Romance from some of the best authors in the business. Without your support, there is no 'us', so we sincerely hope you adore these stories and find some new favorite authors along the way.

Happy Reading!

CEO, Dragonblade Publishing

Publisher's Note

Introduction by Kathryn Le Veque, CEO, Dragonblade Publishing:

When I first conceived of the wild world of the Lyon's Den Connected World, I had a lot of fun with it. I'm a brainstormer. Therefore, to understand just what this world is about, as a reader, then I want to let you in on what the details are. These are the guidelines that every author who has written in the world has gone by. Our first author, Jade Lee, helped me refine the details a little, so here's the scandalous and sexy world of The Lyon's Den:

Regency London: Rich women with scandalous reputations pay the Black Widow of Whitehall to find them wealthy husbands from her gambling den on the West End.

The Black Widow of Whitehall is Mrs. Bessie Dove-Lyon and her gambling establishment is called the Lyon's Den, a front for the rather ruthless matchmaking service. She takes an 'order' from a wealthy woman and then targets the men who come into her establishment, rating them on their viability. If they meet her standards, she will coerce them into the marriage contracts by rigging the games they are playing.

The Lyon's Den isn't a usual gambling establishment – they bet on odd things, like drinking liquor that's been mildly poisoned to see who passes out first, or feeding gluttons too much to see who will vomit first. There are traditional games, but it's more known for its odd and sometimes ruthless games.

Because there are high stakes to be paid out, it lures some of London's finest men. Mrs. Dove-Lyon serves the best wines and alcohol, plus she always has the best food in London. There is a good deal to attract high stakes gamblers and she knows it. Her matchmaking is not a secret and men go willingly to the establishment, some of them looking for a wealthy bride as much as the disreputable women are looking for husbands.

Mrs. Dove-Lyon comes from a very old family, but it was her husband's family who built the house that is home to the Lyon's Den. Located on the west end of London on Cleveland Row, the home was once known as Lyon's Gate Manor and is distinctively painted blue. The truth is that Mrs. Dove-Lyon herself was a woman of questionable repute, rumored to be a former courtesan before she married Colonel Sandstrom T. Lyons, a much older man from a highly respected family. When Colonel Lyons died only a few years into their marriage, Bessie came to see that there was no real money left, only a mountain of debt hidden behind a good family name. But since the house belonged to Mrs. Dove-Lyon, she decided to do what she knew best – and turned it into the most lucrative gambling dens in London. By the time our stories are set, The Lyon's Den has been in existence for about ten years. Mrs. Dove-Lyon is a widow and always wears black, her face shrouded, so no one really knows what she looks like or how old she really is. This makes her mysterious.

And powerful.

Now, dear reader, you know what our authors know heading into the Lyon's Den. I hope this guide shows you just how exciting, dangerous, and diverse the Lyon's Den can be. A truly awesome connected world of wonderful characters and wonderful authors.

Happy Reading!

Contents

Into the Lyon's Den

By Jade Lee

Book #1

Date: (None Given)

Enter the world of the most notorious gambling den in London, where matches are made... unusually. Welcome to the world of THE LYON'S DEN: The Black Widow of Whitehall Connected World, where the underground of Regency London thrives... and loves.

Intrigue makes for strange bedfellows...Elliott, Lord Byrn, often found himself in strange places, but none is more bizarre than the infamous Lyon's Den gaming house in a tony part of London. The gambling doesn't surprise him, nor the salacious things rumored to happen in the upstairs rooms. What shocks him is a slip of a girl jeweler/fence who bargains with him over a missing brooch.

He needs her to refashion the thing before anyone else realizes it is missing and she drives a hard bargain. Harder than he can imagine...Amber Gohar lives her days in the gray world of a gambling hell, but she dreams of escaping into the vibrant world of the ton.

When the opportunity arises for her to spend just one night at a society ball, she grabs it with both hands, never expecting that she would also be taking hold of a man who set her heart on fire. But once she realizes what she's done, she won't let go. She can't. Happily ever after doesn't come easily, or for free, in the world of The Lyon's Den.

Hero:

Elliott Rees – He is the Earl of Byrn, and is in politics.

Heroine:

Amber Gohar – She is a tradeswoman and jeweler at her family's business, the Dragon's Hoard; located within the Lyon's Den

Other Characters:

- Diana Rees Hough – She is Lady Dunnamore, and is married to an elderly man three times her senior.

- Lady Byrn – She is the dowager Countess of Byrn, and is the mother of Elliott, Diana, and Gwen.

- Lady Morthan – She is the dowager Countess of Morthan. Her son is Lord Morthan.

- Lord Morthan – He is the son of the dowager Countess of Morthan. He is the father of Mr. Laurence John.

- Geoffrey Hough – He is the heir of his father, Lord Dunnamore, and is the stepson of Lady Diana Dunnamore. He is an inveterate gambler at the Lyon's Den.

- Christopher Jupp – He is the son and heir of Lord Portham. He is romantically interested in Amber Gohar.

Cast in the Lyon's Den:

- Bessie Dove-Lyon – Mysterious widow, and owner of The Lyon's Den

- Li-Na – Also known as the Abacus Woman. She is from China, and sits next to Amber and her grandfather in their jewelry store, the Dragon's Hoard.

- Hippolyta – She is the pit boss.

- Mr. Gold – He is the father of Amber Gohar, and works in their family business, the Dragon's Hoard.

- Mr. Gold – He is the grandfather of Amber Gohar, and works in their family business, the Dragon's Hoard.

- Joseph – He is newest, youngest apprentice of Mr. Gold, and takes Amber's place in the family jewelry business.

- Titan (Luke) – He is the future Earl of Wolvesmead, and is known as Lord Lucifer. He is the leader of the Wolf Pack of bouncers at the Lyon's Den. He is a scarred war veteran.

- Philostrate – He is a mute guardian at the Lyon's Den.

THE SCANDALOUS LYON

By Maggi Andersen

Book #2

Date: March 1814

Lord Jason Glazebrook has no plans to settle down. He will not inherit for several years, and worse, he is at odds with his brother, Charles, Duke of Shrewsbury, who believes him capable of a dangerous, dishonorable act.

To escape the tension at home, Jason spends many hours at his club, the Lyon's Den in Whitehall. When the unscrupulous match-maker, Mrs. Bessie Dove-Lyon introduces him to a debutante, Miss Beverly Crabtree, Jason considers the beautiful young lady perfect for a dalliance, and invites her to ride with him in Hyde Park. When he discovers Beverly is a gently reared girl, he is determined not to see her again. But he cannot forget her and allows Dove-Lyon to draw him back into her net.

Despite his brother's warning, Jason refuses to relinquish the love-ly Miss Crabtree's company. He senses she is in trouble and wants to help. And much more. He has never met a woman he wanted for his own…until he met Beverly. But so much stands in their way.

It is only a matter of time before shame and disgrace befall the Crabtree family. While her worried mother seeks a wealthy suitor for her, Beverly tries to deny her feelings for Jason. The noble Shrewsbur-ys will never accept her as his wife. Jason's plan may be a possible way out of her troubles. With few options left to her, and the lure of spending days in his company, Beverly is determined to take the chance.

Hero:

Jason Glazebrook, who is the younger brother of Charles Glazebrook, Duke of Shrewsbury.

Heroine:

Beverly Crabtree, the granddaughter of Baron Daintith.

Other Characters:

- Mrs. Crabtree – She is Beverly's mother, and the estranged daughter of Baron Daintith.
- Mr. Crabtree – He is Beverly's father.
- Lord Daintith – He is the grandfather of Beverly Crabtree, and is the 6th Baron Daintith.
- Charles Glazebrook – Older brother of Jason Glazebrook, and the Duke of Shrewsbury.
- Anthony Perlew – He was another suitor for Beverly's hand.
- MaryAnne George – She is Beverly's chaperone.

Cast in the Lyon's Den:

- Bessie Dove-Lyon – She is the mysterious widow of Colonel Sandstrom T. Lyon, and is the proprietress of The Lyon's Den.

FED TO THE LYON

By Mary Lancaster

Book #3

Date: (None Given)

On the day the Princess of Wales goes into exile, Diana loses both her court place and her betrothed. Devastated, she staggers home in the small hours of the morning, alone, drunk—and ruined in the eyes of Society.

In desperation, her mother takes her to the infamous matchmaker, the Black Widow of Whitehall. Abandoned and alone at the scandalous Lyon's Den gaming house, Diana is disguised as a boy and there encounters her prospective groom, wealthy Scottish nobleman, Lord Garvie.

She is appalled.

However, Mrs. Dove-Lyon plays a deep game, and nothing is quite as it seems at the Lyon's Den, where Diana finds unexpected adventure, passion, heartache, and the true love she always dreamed of.

Hero:

William "Bill" Angus, the Earl of Garvie

Heroine:

Diana Wade, a previous lady-of-the-bedchamber for the Princess of Wales.

Other Characters:

- Lady Wade – She is the other of Lady Diana Wade.

- Geoffrey Wade – Lord Wade is the father of Lady Diana Wade.

- Simon Bamber – Lady Diana's former betrothed. He left her to go to the continent with the Princess of Wales.

- Eric Campbell – He is a rich Scotsman, but somewhat of a boor. He is the potential suitor for Lady Diana Wade.

- Mr. Harrington – He is a disreputable gambler at the Lyon's Den, and is a contemporary of Eric Campbell.

Cast in the Lyon's Den:

- Bessie Dove-Lyon – She is the mysterious widow of Colonel Sandstrom T. Lyon, and is the proprietress of The Lyon's Den.

- Titan – He is the head bouncer at the Lyon's Den.

- Lysander – He is the escort at the door of the Lyon's Den.

- Egeus – He is a servant at the Lyon's Den.

THE LYON'S LADY LOVE

By Alexa Aston

Book #4

Date: April 1816

Can an earl put aside the ghosts of the past and accept a future with his scandal-plagued wife?

On the night of her come-out, Lady Emma Spencer learns her father has bilked numerous peers. Not only is she humiliated, but her father flees England, leaving Emma penniless and homeless. She finds work as a companion and years later, she winds up with a fortune. All she lacks now is the children she so desperately desires. That means finding a husband—and she turns to The Black Widow of Whitehall, Mrs. Bessie Dove-Lyon, who pairs women touched by scandal with men in desperate need of money.

Upon his father's death, Marcus becomes the Earl of Rutherford and finds he's bankrupt, thanks to his father losing the family fortune to poor investments and gambling. Though Marcus had wanted to wed for love, he turns to an infamous matchmaker, who arranges a marriage for him. Lady Emma Spencer is everything he dreamed of in a woman, and Marcus gallantly refuses to discuss her past, telling Emma he is her future. But secrets have a way of coming out and Marcus learns he's married to the one woman he never would have chosen. Can Marcus put aside the ghosts of the past and accept a future with his wife?

Hero:

Marcus Powell, the Earl of Rutherford.

Heroine:

Emma Spencer, the daughter of Lord Seton.

Cast of Characters:

- Marcus Powell – Hero of THE LYON'S LADY LOVE. He is the Earl of Rutherford.

- Emma Spencer – Heroine of THE LYON'S LADY LOVE. She is the daughter of Lord Seton.

- Lady Amanda Stanley – She is the sister of Marcus Powell, Earl of Rutherford.

- Lord Stanley – He is the husband of Lady Amanda Stanley.

- Florence Blackwell – She is the widow of Major Blackwell, and had hired Lady Emma Spencer to be he companion, after Lord Seton abandoned his daughter. She is also the older sister of Bessie Dove-Lyon.

- Lord Seton – He is the father of Lady Emma Spencer. He is a swindler, and escaped his victims by leaving England. He left his daughter behind to fend for herself.

- Lady Seton – She is the second wife of Lord Seton, the stepmother to Lady Emma Spencer.

- Jeremy St. Clair – He is the Duke of Everton, and the husband of Catherine St. Clair.

- Catherine St. Clair – She is the Duchess of Everton, and is married to Jeremy St. Clair.

- Luke St. Clair – He is the Earl of Mayfield, and is married to Caroline St. Clair, the Countess of Mayfield.

- Caroline St. Clair – She is the Countess of Mayfield, and is married to Luke St. Clair.

- Laurel St. Clair – She is the illegitimate half-sister of Jeremy St. Clair and Luke St. Clair.
- Evan Drake – He is the Marquess of Merrick, and is married to Rachel Drake.
- Rachel Drake – She is the Marchioness of Merrick, and is married to Evan Drake.

Cast in the Lyon's Den:

- Bessie Dove-Lyon – She is the mysterious widow of Colonel Sandstrom T. Lyon, and is the proprietress of The Lyon's Den. She is also the youngest sister of Florence Blackwell.
- Lysander – He is the escort at the door of the Lyon's Den.
- Egeus – He is a wolf at the door of the Lyon's Den.
- Demetrius – He is a bouncer at the door of the Lyon's Den.
- Philostrate – He is a bouncer at the Lyon's Den.
- Hippolyta – She is the pit boss at the Lyon's Den.
- Puck – He is a bouncer at the Lyon's Den.
- Hermia – She is a wolf at the Lyon's Den.
- Theseus – He is a wolf at the Lyon's Den.

THE LYON'S LAIRD

By Hildie McQueen

Book #5

Date: (None Given)

After being caught in the most embarrassing of situations that leaves her with a permanent limp, Evangeline Prescott's reputation is beyond repair, and so her mother takes it upon herself to approach the Widow of Whitehall in an attempt to find her a suitable husband.

In London for a short season, Scottish Laird Camren Maclean accepts an intriguing invitation to a prestigious gambling den where he loses a high stakes card game. The price of his loss is for him to marry a stranger within a week. A beautiful socialite, a handsome Laird, and a game of chance. Can anyone win?

Hero:

Camren Maclean, Laird of Clan Maclean.

Heroine:

Evangeline Prescott, the spinster daughter of wealthy parents, Forest and Olivia Prescott.

Other Characters:

- Forest Prescott – He is the father of Evangeline, and is an actuary.

- Olivia Prescott – She is the mother of Evangeline, and is the sister of Lady Fern Monroe.

- Lord Monroe – He is the brother-in-law to Olivia Prescott, and is the father of Prudence.

- Lady Fern Monroe – She is the mother of Prudence, and is the sister of Olivia Prescott.

- Miss Prudence – She is Evangeline Prescott's first cousin, and is the daughter of Lord and Lady Monroe.

- Rose Edwards – She is the best friend of Evangeline Prescott. She is interested in Gideon Sutherland.

- Gideon Sutherland – He is a fellow clansman in Clan Maclean, and has traveled to London with Cameron for the whiskey distribution center they oversee. He has won a townhome in London, courtesy of Mrs. Bessie Dove-Lyon. He is also interested in Rose Edwards.

- Avery Hamilton – He is the former lover of Evangeline Prescott.

- Mortimer Witt – He is a business associate of Mr. Prescott, and was a possible suitor for Evangeline Prescott's hand.

- Mariel Maclean – She is Camren's mother.

- Ian Maclean – He is Camren's brother, and husband to Sencha Maclean.

- Sencha Maclean – She is Ian Maclean's wife.

- Adele Maclean – She is Camren's sister.

- Cowan Maclean – He is the younger brother of Camren and Ian Maclean, and is known as the pirate in the family. He is quick to temper.

Cast in the Lyon's Den:

- Bessie Dove-Lyon – She is the mysterious widow of Colonel Sandstrom T. Lyon, and is the proprietress of The Lyon's Den. She is also the youngest sister of Florence Blackwell.

THE LYON SLEEPS TONIGHT

By Elizabeth Ellen Carter

Book #6

Date: (None Given)

Love is just a whim away. Free-spirited Opal Jones and straight-laced Peter Ravenshaw are childhood friends growing up in India, away from the structured mores of English society. But all good things must come to an end. The friends are sent to England and go their separate ways.

Years pass but not Opal's love for Peter. Opal is determined to get her man, but she will need the help of Lady Dove-Lyon, the most notorious matchmaker in London.

The Lyon's Den will host a most unusual game: He who can stay awake the longest, wins the hand of the fair Miss Opal Jones. Peter is horrified that his beautiful, headstrong friend would give herself away on a game of chance, not realizing that Opal already holds all the cards.

Hero:

Peter Ravenshaw, former captain in the army; now retired. Childhood friend of Opal Jones.

Heroine:

Opal Jones, daughter of a former major in the army. Childhood friend of Peter Ravenshaw.

Other Characters:

- Sinclair Jones – Former major in the army. He is the father of Opal Jones.
- Beatrice Jones – Mother of Opal Jones.
- Mrs. Ravenshaw – Mother of Peter Ravenshaw.
- Miles Rutherford – Earl of Harcourt, and one of the "Brothers Bachelor."
- Amber Honeyfield – Former fiancé of Miles Rutherford.
- Oliver Kettering – Viscount Roxbury, and one of the "Brothers Bachelor."
- Winston Evans – He is an MP for the Berkshire district, and friend and neighbor to Peter Ravenshaw.

Cast in the Lyon's Den:

- Bessie Dove-Lyon – She is the Black Widow of Whitehall, and the proprietor of the Lyon's Den.
- Heleus – He is in charge of the attendants at the Lyon's Den.
- Themisto – She is a servant at the Lyon's Den.

A Lyon in Her Bed

By Amanda Mariel

Book #7

Date: 1814

A woman seeking escape…Lady Emiline Hawthorne will do anything to avoid an unwanted union—even marry a stranger. To that end, she goes to The Lyon's Den to enlist Mrs. Bessie Dove-Lyon's help. There is only one problem; Emiline cannot pay the matchmaking fee.

A man with a broken heart…Leonard Quinton, 6th Earl of Morton, returned from war to discover everyone he loved had betrayed him. Now he must beget an heir without risking his heart. He proposes a simple arrangement to the first lady he sees at The Lyon's Den—The use of her womb in return for his financial support.

Two souls, one heart…When Emiline finds the old Countess of Morton's diary, she learns the secrets of Leonard's past. Secrets even he does not know.

Hero:

Leonard "Leo" Quinton, 6th Earl of Moreton

Heroine:

Emiline Hawthorne, daughter of a physician

Other Characters:

- Mrs. Hawthorne – She is Emiline's mother.

- Mary Quinton – Eldest child and daughter of Leo and Emiline Quinton.

- George Quinton – Second child and heir of Leo and Emeline Quinton.

Cast in the Lyon's Den:

- Bessie Dove-Lyon – She is the Black Widow of Whitehall, and the proprietor of the Lyon's Den.

FALL OF THE LYON

By Chasity Bowlin

Book #8

Date: February 1814

Faced with the devastating and impending loss of her stepfather and the all too real threat of unscrupulous relatives who would have her inheritance at any cost, Miss Margaret Upshaw flees to London. Her stepfather has tasked her to make her way to the Lyon's Den to seek the assistance of Mrs. Bessie Dove-Lyon, the most scandalous matchmaker in all of London. Her matches aren't made in the ballrooms of Mayfair, but over the faro tables and a notorious betting book in the gaming hell she rules with an iron fist in a velvet glove.

Leander Thurston-Hunter, Viscount Amberley, or Leo as he prefers, is a man with a very particular problem that can only be solved with money. And as a nobleman, there's only one way to get a lot of cash and get it quickly—you have to marry it. When Mrs. Dove-Lyon informs him that she's made the perfect match for him, he's not exactly thrilled, but certainly willing to do his duty to preserve his family's standing. But then he meets Meg Upshaw. Beautiful, vulnerable, terribly alone… and she makes him question for the first time whether a marriage born out of duty and necessity has to be an unhappy one.

But there's one terrible catch… Meg's family, the relatives who would have her fortune by any means, are the very ones responsible for the brutal events that nearly ended his life and left him permanently scarred. But that isn't the only secret they're keeping, and those secrets are worth dying for and worth killing for. Leo and his new bride find themselves in danger of far more than simply falling inconveniently in love.

Hero:

Leander "Leo" Thurston-Hunter, Viscount Amberley

Heroine:

Margaret Upshaw, stepdaughter of Sir William Ashby

Other Characters:
- William Ashby – He is the stepfather of Margaret Upshaw, and is the half-brother of Roger Snead.
- Roger Snead – He is the half-brother of Sir William Ashby, and is the father of Neville Snead.
- Neville Snead – He is the son of Roger Snead, and is the nephew of Sir William Ashby.
- Miles Herndon – He is Lord Armstrong, and is a friend to Leo Thurston-Hunter.
- Julia Thurston-Hunter – She is a half-sister to Leo Thurston-Hunter.
- Louisa Thurston-Hunter – She is a half-sister to Leo Thurston-Hunter.

Cast in the Lyon's Den:
- Bessie Dove Lyon   She is the Black Widow of Whitehall, and the proprietor of the Lyon's Den.

LYON'S PREY

By Anna St. Clair

Book #9

Date: December 1816

Haunted by his wife's death, he vowed to never marry again...until he meets her! Evan Prescott, the fifth Earl of Clarendon lost his wife during the birth of their child. Broken, Evan seeks solace in the Lyon's Den, a world of drink, cards, and excess—where wins and losses are easier to navigate than responsibilities. Overconfident and in his cups, he makes a bet that will change his life.

Still mourning the loss of her father and elder brother, Lady Charlotte Grisham saves her young brother from the path of a speeding carriage. In a fit of pique, she throws propriety to the wind and storms up the steps of the owner's London townhouse—and meets the man that upends her world.

The stars align when his high stakes bet and her lapse in judgement give the Black Widow of Whitehall the perfect opportunity to spin her web of hearts, while untold danger lurks a step behind.

Hero:

Evan Prescott, 5th Earl of Clarendon

Heroine:

Charlotte Grisham, daughter of Lord and Lady Romney

Other Characters:

- Amelia Prescott – She's the first wife of Evan Prescott, and she died giving birth to Evan's son and heir, Edward Prescott.

- Edward Prescott – He's the first son and heir of Evan Prescott and his first wife, Amelia Prescott.

- Dowager Countess of Clarendon – She is the mother of Evan Prescott and Lady Catherine Rivers.

- Lady Catherine Rivers – She's the sister of Evan Prescott, and is married to Lord Rivers.

- Lord Tom Rivers – He's the husband of Lady Catherine Rivers, and the brother-in-law of Evan Prescott.

- Christopher Anglesey – He is the Earl of Banbury, and is a friend to Evan Prescott.

- Lady Romney – She is Lady Charlotte Grisham's mother. Her late husband, Lord Romney, was a good friend to Bessie Dove-Lyon's late husband, Colonel Sandstrom T. Lyon.

- Jason Grisham – He is the young presumptive heir to the Earl of Romney, as his older brother, Matthew Grisham, is missing in the Americas.

- Baron Langdale – He is Lady Romney's brother, and is was a temporary guardian for young Jason Grisham.

Cast in the Lyon's Den:

- Bessie Dove-Lyon – She is the Black Widow of Whitehall, and the proprietor of the Lyon's Den. She is a friend to Lady Romney, as her late husband, Lord Romney, was a friend to Bessie Dove-Lyon's late husband, Colonel Sandstrom T. Lyon.

- Titan (AKA Luke Cross) – He is a bouncer at the Lyon's Den.

LOVED BY THE LYON

By Collette Cameron

Book #10

Date: March 1816

Kingston Barclay cannot inherit the dukedom soon enough. With siblings to support and a nearly bankrupt estate, an opportune marriage is his last hope. But his best-laid plans are upended when he discovers his best friend's lovely sister sneaking around the Lyon's Den. His immediate attraction to her would make her a most inconvenient bride, given his circumstances. Convincing his heart of that, however, is another matter entirely…

The last thing Vanessa Becket needs is another man in her life. Between her conniving stepbrother, a parade of fortune hunters, and the investigator who failed to reclaim her stolen jewels, she's had enough. But when she finds herself in a notorious gaming hell, she discovers something far more valuable than missing gems. A temporary arranged marriage to Kingston could solve all her problems. If she manages to not fall for him in the process, that is… It was supposed to be a simple arrangement. But given their histories—and the secrets Kingston is keeping—the road to happily ever after will surely be anything but simple.

Hero:

Kingston Barclay, who later becomes the Duke of Caerleon

Heroine:

Vanessa Becket, wealthy heiress, and younger sister of Kingston Barclay's late best friend

Other Characters:

- Owen Elligon – He's the stepbrother of Vanessa Becket.
- Pierce Chamberlain – He's the Earl of Wainthorpe, and is a friend to Kingston Barclay.
- Crispin Rolston – He is the Duke of Bainbridge, and is a friend to Kingston Barclay.
- Stanford Bancroft – He is the Duke of Asherford, and is a friend to Kingston Barclay.
- Madeline Barclay – She is the younger sister of Kingston Barclay.
- Rebecca Barclay – She is the younger sister of Kingston Barclay.
- Dorena Barclay – She is the younger sister of Kingston Barclay.
- Gareth Barclay – He is the younger brother of Kingston Barclay.
- Paxton Barclay – He is the younger brother of Kingston Barclay.

Cast in the Lyon's Den:

- Bessie Dove-Lyon – She is the Black Widow of Whitehall, and the proprietor of the Lyon's Den.
- Egeus – He is a bouncer at the Lyon's Den.
- Theseus – He is a bouncer at the Lyon's Den.

THE LYON'S DEN IN WINTER

By Whitney Blake

Book #11

Date: December 1814

Viola Black is not conventional—she dresses as a man to sell her sought-after plays to London companies. She's lucky. Her father, wily solicitor Malcolm Black, turns a benevolent blind eye to her habits. That is, until one frigid night, when she's cornered by ruffians. While Viola tries to dismiss the incident as a hazard of London life, Papa is more alarmed. She senses there is far more he's not telling her. But she's keeping something to herself, too.

Though she was shaken by her attack, she also had the good fortune of running into Dr. Duncan Neilson—whom she can't banish from her head. When Papa insists the Black Widow of Whitehall find her a husband, Viola balks. None of the eligible bachelors will be the magnetic Dr. Neilson, for a start. Then he walks into the Black Widow's parlor, charming and enigmatic as ever. But before the two can benefit from fate or providence, Viola is abducted and becomes entangled in an old feud she knew nothing about.

Papa has been concealing his past from her, and it involves the same underworld as the Black Widow's. As Viola keeps a level head and contemplates escape, her unexpected fiancée is working with her father to bring her home. Does love wait for her on the other side of intrigue and deception? She dearly wants to find out, and she's certain that even her plays are less dramatic than all this.

Hero:

Duncan Neilson, a widowed physician based in Scotland

Heroine:

Viola Black, daughter of Malcolm Black, and a writer of plays

Other Characters:

- Malcolm Black – He's the father of Viola Black, and is a former lover of Bessie Dove-Lyon. They are still good friends. Malcolm is also a solicitor by day, and a consulting card sharp at night. He is also known as the Silver Tongue.

- Watson – Dr. Watson is a fellow physician and colleague of Duncan Neilson. He lives in England.

- Constance Neilson – She is the daughter of Duncan Neilson and his late wife, Amelia Neilson.

- Everett – He is a former colleague of Malcolm Black, and is now his enemy.

- Mr. Barney – He is the kidnapper and thug hired by Everett to kidnap Viola Black.

Cast in the Lyon's Den:

- Bessie Dove-Lyon – She is the Black Widow of Whitehall, and the proprietor of the Lyon's Den. In this story, she's a former lover of Malcolm Black, and still a good friend of his.

KISS OF THE LYON

By Meara Platt

Book #12

Date: May 1817

He was only supposed to win the high stakes game of chance, not a bride along with it. Lord Matthew Lyon is often called upon by the Crown because of his mathematical brilliance, and participating in a high stakes game of chance at the notorious Lyon's Den should have been the easy part of his assignment…only it goes terribly wrong. He wins the pot, as expected since his probability calculations never fail. But no one calculated on his winning the hand of Lady Danielle Haverfield, daughter of the Earl of Haverfield, the prime suspect in a treason plot against the Crown and the very man he is assigned to bring down.

She was only trying to stop her brother from gambling his life away. Lady Danielle Haverfield knew she did not belong in the Lyon's Den, but she had to stop her brother before he gambled away his entire inheritance. Not only did she fail to stop him, but she's ruined her life as well. Lady Dove-Lyon will not allow her brother to go unpunished, even though the handsome Scottish lord who's wiped him out is willing to forgive the debt. But the Black Widow of Whitehall has a fearsome reputation to maintain. Someone is going to have to pay for her brother's inability to pay up, and she's decided it is to be Danielle. Well, the handsome Scot could have asked for her only for the one night, but he's proposed marriage instead. Can their love survive his secrets and her father's betrayal?

<u>Meet Matthew's brothers:</u>

Cheyne Lyon – The Lyon's Surprise

Lucas Lyon – Lyon in the Rough

Hero:

Matthew Lyon, brother of the Duke of Mar, and a professor of mathematics at the University of Edinburgh

Heroine:

Danielle Haverfield, daughter of the Earl of Haverfield, and sister of Viscount Royston

Other Characters:

- Simon Haverfield – He is Viscount Royston, and is the older brother of Danielle Haverfield.
- Earl of Haverfield – He is the father of Simon and Danielle Haverfield.
- Josiah Haverfield – He is the younger brother of the Earl of Haverfield.
- Duke of Lotheil – He is the chairman of the Royal Society.
- Lord Manning – He is the person in charge of the Home Office.
- Homer Barrow – He is a Bow Street Runner, and also does work for the Duke of Lotheil.
- Lily Farthingale – She is an attendee at the Royal Society, who listened to the lecture given by Professor Lyon.

Cast in the Lyon's Den:

- Bessie Dove-Lyon – She is the Black Widow of Whitehall, and the proprietor of the Lyon's Den. In this story, Matthew Lyon's granduncle was Sandstrom Lyon. They are related.

ALWAYS THE LYON TAMER

By Emily E K Murdoch

Book #13

Date: (None Given)

Always taming gentlemen but never getting her own – but the Lyon's Den will change that. Miss Rebecca Darby is tired of being courted by John Lennox, Marquis of Gloucester. After months of empty promises, it's time to take matters into her own hands. Because John 'the Lion' Lennox is always surrounded by his pride of ladies, and she's never able to get close.

His flirting has led nowhere, and Rebecca won't stand for it anymore. Not when the Lyon's Den, the secretive club owned by Mrs. Dove-Lyon, promises to play games leading to happy matrimony. John has no idea what faces him in the game. Rebecca has no idea whether her shyness will allow her to carry through with her plans, but if she doesn't try, she'll always wonder.

He doesn't recognize the mysterious woman in the mask. She knows this is her only chance to tame him. In a world where women rule the roost and gentlemen must do what they're told, it will take a Lyon Tamer to bring John to his knees. But once the masks are removed, will Rebecca have her way, or will the Lyon escape into the night?

Hero:

John Lennox, Marquess of Gloucester, and the brother of the Duke of Mercia. He is also known as the "Lion of the Lennoxes."

Heroine:

Rebecca Darby, who has been dating John Lennox for a couple of years

Other Characters:

- Mr. Darby – He is Rebecca Darby's elderly father.
- William Lennox – He is the Duke of Mercia, and is the older brother of John Lennox.
- Charlotte Lennox – She is the Duchess of Mercia, and the wife of William Lennox.
- Prudence Lennox – She is the younger sister of William Lennox and John Lennox.

Cast in the Lyon's Den:

- Bessie Dove-Lyon – She is the Black Widow of Whitehall, and the proprietor of the Lyon's Den.
- Hermia – She is an employee at the Lyon's Den.

TO TAME THE LYON

By Sky Purington

Book #14

Date: 1815

Can a woman and her daughter heal the broken heart of a grieving man? Or will ghosts of old keep him forever distanced? When her rake of a husband promises her to another before he dies, Clara Ainsworth, Duchess of Surrey, has no choice but to seek out matchmaker Mrs. Dove-Lyon and the protection of another marriage. More so, she must trick her childhood love, Isaac, into a union, not just for her sake, but his.

At one time, he had been there for her, so she's determined to return the favor and see him free of his self-destructive ways. Having suffered more loss than most, Isaac MacLauchlin, Marquess of Durham, frequents the Lyon's Den to drown his grief in liquor. Or so he leads others to believe. In truth, he's keeping tabs on his lost love, Clara. So imagine his surprise when she tricks him into a marriage contract to avoid the results of a pre-duel agreement. Naturally, he will protect her, but marrying her is another story. It might come at too high a risk to his wounded heart.

Hero:

Isaac MacLauchlin, Marquess of Durham

Heroine:

Clara Ainsworth, formerly the Duchess of Surrey

Other Characters:

- Andrew MacLauchlin – He was the late older brother of Isaac MacLauchlin.
- Blake MacLauchlin – He's the Scottish cousin of Isaac MacLauchlin, and is Viscount Lorne. He prefers to go by Lord MacLauchlin.
- Mabel Ainsworth – She is the only child of the late Duke of Surrey and his wife, the Duchess of Surrey; Clara Ainsworth.
- Maude – She's the previous wet nurse, teacher, friend, and lady's maid to the Duchess of Surrey. Later she marries Blake MacLauchlin and becomes Lady MacLauchlin.
- Lord Kent – He fought a duel with and fatally wounded the Duke of Surrey.

Cast in the Lyon's Den:

- Bessie Dove-Lyon – She is the Black Widow of Whitehall, and the proprietor of the Lyon's Den.

HOW TO STEAL A LYON'S FORTUNE

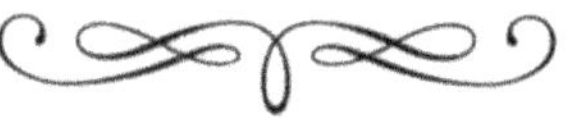

By Alanna Lucas

Book #15

Date: (None Given)

When it comes to stealing a Lyon's fortune, it takes two to right a wrong. Visitors to the Lyon's Den, run by the mysterious Mrs. Dove-Lyon, usually wish to find a spouse, but Audrey has quite another goal in mind. She needs help to secure an invitation to Lyon's masquerade, the annual event hosted by her once-stepfather, Vincent Lyon, so that she may retrieve the statue he stole from her late mother.

Mrs. Dove-Lyon knows just the person to take Audrey to the ball, a shrewd matchmaker that she is, also sees an opportunity to help Lord Peter Dermott, who has been recommended to her as being in urgent need of a wife. When Peter meets Audrey, the attraction is instant, but she presents him with a huge dilemma. Her plan to take the statue is daring, and if it fails, his reputation will be ruined.

Hero:

Peter Dermott, Guardian of his young sister and niece, honorable head of his household with the title of a baron

Heroine:

Audrey Ruston, former stepdaughter of Vincent Lyon, who was the nephew of the late Sandstrom Lyon; husband of Bessie Dove-Lyon

Cast of Characters:

- Louis de Coucy – He is the uncle of Audrey Ruston, and is the brother of her late mother. He is a painter, procurer, and collector of art.

- Vincent Lyon – He was the former stepfather of Audrey Royston, and is the nephew of the late Sandstrom Lyon (husband to Bessie Dove-Lyon).

- Leona Dermott – She is the younger sister of Peter Dermott.

- Kitty – She is the young niece of Peter Dermott.

- Mr. Leyland – He's the wealthy American who wants to purchase a valuable statue from its rightful owner, Audrey Ruston.

- Lord Kenwreck – He is the husband of Lady Kenwreck.

- Lady Kenwreck – She is the wife of Lord Kenwreck, and is the sponsor of the Home for Desolate Ladies.

- Lord Bradshaw – He is the oldest friend of Peter Dermott.

Cast in the Lyon's Den:

- Bessie Dove-Lyon – She is the Black Widow of Whitehall, and the proprietor of the Lyon's Den. In this novel, her late husband's nephew, Vincent Lyon, is the protagonist. A nude painting of her during her days as a courtesan is part of this wicked tale.

THE LYON'S SURPRISE

By Meara Platt

Book #16

Date: August 1816

He was an agitated beast, a Lyon of Mar. THE Lyon of Mar.

Cheyne Lyon, Duke of Mar is at first surprised when his wastrel brother dumps a wife and baby on his doorstep. But Jennifer is intelligent, nurturing, and sweet, just the sort Cheyne could love, if only she wasn't already taken. When unsavory strangers come around looking for a runaway young lady, Cheyne realizes Jennifer is not who she claims to be…and he isn't about to give her up.

NOTE: The Lyon's Surprise was formerly published as The Duke's Surprise and has updated content.

<u>Meet Cheyne's brothers:</u>

Matthew Lyon – Kiss of the Lyon

Lucas Lyon – Lyon in the Rough

Hero:

Cheyne Lyon, Duke of Mar, and older brother to Matthew, Lucas, and John

Heroine:

Jenny Bramwell, daughter of an Oxford professor, and best friend of Jenny Bradford Lyon

Other Characters:

- Johnny Lyon – He is the firstborn son of John Lyon and his wife Jenny Bradford Lyon.
- Duchess Davina – She is a childhood friend, whom Cheyne Lyon was considering marriage to.
- Matthew Lyon – He's the hero of KISS OF THE LYON, and is the younger brother of Cheyne Lyon. He is a math professor at the University of Edinburgh.
- Lucas Lyon – He's the younger brother of Cheyne Lyon.
- John Lyon – He is the younger brother of Cheyne Lyon. He is married to Jenny Bradford Lyon, and are parents of Johnny Lyon.
- Jenny Bradford Lyon – She is married to John Lyon, and is the mother of Johnny Lyon.
- Arden Bramwell – He is the uncle to Jenny Bramwell.
- Lord Finster – He is a potential suitor to Jenny Bramwell, through her Uncle Arden Bramwell's machinations.

Cast in the Lyon's Den:

- Bessie Dove-Lyon – She is the Black Widow of Whitehall, and the proprietor of the Lyon's Den. In this novel, her late husband was the granduncle of the Lyon of Mar family – Cheyne, Matthew, Lucas, and John Lyon.

A LYON'S PRIDE

By Emily Royal

Book #17

Date: August 1816

Pride tore them apart—can forgiveness reunite them? On the death of his father, Mason Redstone returns from the militia to claim his title, only to discover his family estate is nearing bankruptcy. He needs money, and he needs it quickly. What better means to secure it than a rich wife, courtesy of Mrs. Dove-Lyon? Having loved, and lost, in his youth, a marriage of convenience is the solution to his problems.

Lily Diamond has known known poverty and hardship, and now runs a successful insurance enterprise. Having hardened her heart after her childhood sweetheart abandoned her a decade ago, she's looking for a titled husband to give her daughters the position in society which was denied her. When she calls upon her mother's old friend, Bessie Dove-Lyon for help in finding a match, she stipulates that the suitor must have no expectations regarding love, or the marriage bed.

When Lily's prospective suitors take part in one of Mrs. Dove-Lyon's games, the Black Widow of Whitehall weaves her spell once more, then presents Lily with her betrothed—the very last man on earth she thought she'd see again. Can Mason prove to Lily that he's conquered the pride which tore them apart? And will Lily trust him enough to reveal the secret she's been keeping for ten years?

<u>The Redstone Family</u>

Lily and Mason in A Lyon's Pride

Mina and Duncan in Lyon of the Highlands

Hero:

Mason Redstone, the Earl of Redstone

Heroine:

Lily Diamond, formerly de Viliers, daughter of a baron on his family's estate

Other Characters:

- Francesca de Viliers – She's the widow of a baronet, and is the mother of Lily Diamond. She also was "La Flamme," a famous courtesan at the Lyon's Den.
- Amelia Diamond – She's the illegitimate twin daughter of Lily Diamond and Mason Redstone.
- Belinda Diamond – She's the illegitimate twin daughter of Lily Diamond and Mason Redstone.
- Wilhelmina Redstone – She's the stepmother to Mason Redstone, and is the dowager Countess of Redstone.
- Dexter Hart – He's a banker, and is a friend to Mason Redstone.
- William Dawkins – He's the Marquess of Easton, and is a friend to Mason Redstone.
- Henry Drayton – He's the Duke of Westbury, and is a neighbor to the Redstones.
- Jeanette Drayton – She's the Duchess of Westbury, and is a neighbor to the Redstones.

Cast in the Lyon's Den:

- Bessie Dove-Lyon – She is the Black Widow of Whitehall, and the proprietor of the Lyon's Den. In this novel, she is friends with

Lady Francesca de Villiers, formerly a baronet's widow, but who later becomes a courtesan at the Lyon's Den.

- Hermia – She is a serving attendant at the Lyon's Den.

LYON EYES

By Lynne Connolly

Book #18

Date: February 1815

Heiress to a fortune, Jenny Hambling needs a husband, before she is made to marry a man she despises. The Lyon's Den is her only option to buy a husband fast. But she runs into the last man she wants to meet, Miles, The Duke of Goldthorpe. He ruined Jenny's debut by calling her a Mill Girl. Now he will ruin her bargain with his friend.

Three years ago, Miles saw Jenny and tumbled head over heels in love. Doubting his feelings, he called her a name he later regretted, but he arrived at her house too late to apologize. Jenny had gone home. Philosophically, Miles put the whole incident down to a brief infatuation and went on with his life. But infuriatingly, he could never forget her. Now, he can do no less than make amends for her disastrous first season.

Thrown together, Jenny and Miles find their attraction as strong as ever. But their lives have moved on, and they find themselves in a new place. Miles is a duke with all the pomp and responsibility that entails. Jenny has an industrial empire to manage in the north. The obstacles seem too great. But are they really?

Hero:

Miles, Duke of Goldthorpe

Heroine:

Jenny Hambling, wealthy heiress of her father's mill business

Other Characters:

- Cecilia – She's the sister of Miles, Duke of Goldthorpe.

- Dowager – She's the dowager Duchess of Goldthorpe, and is the mother of Miles and Cecilia.

- Francis "Frank" Burrell – He is a captain in the 8th Dragoons, and is a friend of Miles.

- Wilfred Kelly – He owns a small percentage of the mill business that Jenny Hambling's father's business. He is pursuing Jenny Hambling to marry him.

- _______ Winwood – She is Lady Costerbridge, and is the mother of Juliet Winwood.

- _______ Winwood – He is Lord Costerbridge, and is the father of Juliet Winwood.

- Juliet Winwood – She is the daughter of Lord and Lady Costerbridge, and was hoping to be the next Duchess of Goldthorpe.

Cast in the Lyon's Den:

- Bessie Dove-Lyon – She is the Black Widow of Whitehall, and the proprietor of the Lyon's Den.

- Pyramus – He's a bouncer at the Lyon's Den.

TAMED BY THE LYON

By Chasity Bowlin

Book #19

Date: March 1814

It was their first kiss, possibly her first kiss ever. All the more reason to get it right. Abandoned at the altar by her groom in favor of her younger sister, Miss Madeline Keyes has become an object of pity, scorn and scandal. Rather than flee to the countryside to rusticate as a spinster with her less than loving parents, she seeks the aid of Mrs. Bessie Dove-Lyon to snare a titled husband and, through marriage, reclaim her place in society.

Lord Oliver Easton, Earl of Foxmore, has always preferred plants to people. As a younger son, he had no expectations of marriage. But with the loss of both his father and brother in a very short span of time, the death taxes levied on the estate leave him at risk of losing his life's work. So he does the only sensible thing and takes his brother's place in the matchmaking scheme helmed by the owner of the Lyon's Den. It was supposed to be a marriage of convenience only. A chance to rescue her reputation and his fortunes. But neither of them expected the ultimate complication—to fall in love.

Hero:

Oliver Thurston, Earl of Foxmore

Heroine:

Madeline Keyes, daughter of William Keyes

Other Characters:

- William Keyes – He's the father of Madeline Keyes and Coraline Keyes, and the husband of Alice Keyes.

- Alice Keyes – She's the stepmother of Madeline and Coraline.

- Coraline Keyes Wortham – She's the younger sister of Madeline Keyes.

- Edmund Keyes – He was formerly betrothed to Madeline Keyes, but married Coraline Keyes instead.

- Leander Thurston-Hunter – He is the hero of FALL OF THE LYON, and is Viscount Amberley.

- Margaret Thurston-Hunter – She is the heroine of FALL OF THE LYON, and is Viscountess Amberley.

Cast in the Lyon's Den:

- Bessie Dove-Lyon – She is the Black Widow of Whitehall, and the proprietor of the Lyon's Den.

LYON HEARTED

By Jade Lee

Book #20

Date: (None Given)

Enter the world of the most notorious gambling den in London, where matches are made... unusually. Welcome to the world of THE LYON'S DEN: The Black Widow of Whitehall Connected World, where the underground of Regency London thrives... and loves.

ABACAS WOMAN

Li-Na lives in a black and white world, painting her feelings onto canvas by day and counting money in the Lyon's Den at night. She's found safety in the dark ink and the heavy clack of her abacas, but it is really a life?

MAN OF ART

Lord Daniel can't draw worth a damn, but he can sell what he finds. And what he finds is Li-Na, a woman of such sublime talent that he will go to extraordinary measures to capture her art. When she refuses to leave her safe cocoon, he conspires with Mrs. Dove-Lyons to bring her to Cornwall where she will have everything she needs to paint.

And if her art requires a more personal connection, then he willingly offers up himself as inspiration.

A SLOW SEDUCTION

Li-Na will not give up her soul to this powerful man, no matter how many castles he owns. She paints him as a tiger hunting in the jungle. She feels him watching her, protecting her, and tempting her until her canvas is filled with his eyes, his mouth, and his caress. But she cannot surrender the only part of her still alive. Unless being consumed by him is the only way to bring color back to her heart.

Hero:

Lord Daniel is the second son of the Earl of Walden. He is also an art collector and dealer, and is friends with Prinny.

Heroine:

Li-Na is also known as the mysterious Abacus Woman in the Lyon's Den. She is from China and was formerly a slave there. In Book #1, she was also the "pretend mistress" to Baron Easterly.

Other Characters:

- Prinny – He's the Prince Regent of England, and is also known as "Prinny." He is also a friend of Lord Daniel, and purchases art from him.

- Nessie – She is the dowager Countess of Walden, and is the mother of Joseph and Stefan, the current Earl of Walden. She is also the sister-in-law of Lord Daniel.

- Joseph – He is the youngest son of Nessie and the late Peder, former Earl of Walden.

- Stefan – He is the oldest son and heir of Nessie and the late Peder, who was the former Earl of Walden. Stefan inherits his late father's title upon his death.

- Lord Lerwich – He is a reprobate, and is a friend of Prinny.
- Lord Gordon – He is the father of Nessie, the dowager Countess of Walden. He is trying to obtain guardianship of his grandson, the Earl of Walden.

Cast in the Lyon's Den:

- Bessie Dove-Lyon – Mysterious black widow, and owner of The Lyon's Den. In this novel, she's the best friend of Li-Na. Mrs. Dove-Lyon gave Li-Na her freedom when she won her from a ship captain in a card game.

THE DEVILISH LYON

By Charlotte Wren

Book #21

Date: September 1816

Mrs. Dove-Lyon, proprietor of the Lyon's Den, London's notorious gaming hell, has recently had dealings with three new clients:

Miss Harriet Hurst, who cannot see a thing without her spectacles and who has an unfortunate aversion to strong perfume, is in search of a husband. Her proposal, however, is a little unorthodox.

Ambrose Crossley, fifth Earl of Pendlewood, an upstanding and respected member of the ton, is in search of a wife. His quest, however, is not quite as straightforward as it seems.

Edward Fortescue, Viscount Eskdale, aka the Fallen Angel of Mayfair, has no desire to marry at all. His request is somewhat unusual.

Being a shrewd businesswoman, Mrs. Dove-Lyon reckons she can satisfy all their needs in one fell swoop. It will require a little bit of subterfuge, a fair amount of manipulation, and a whole heap of good intentions. But, if the gamble pays off, a happy ending for all is assured. The game starts out well, with everything going exactly as planned. But, just as things seem to be reaching a satisfactory conclusion, a tragic secret emerges from the past. The consequences are heartbreaking. The game, it seems, is up. Or is it? True love never surrenders without a fight. And time, it is said, heals all wounds. Maybe there's still a chance for happiness, after all.

Hero:

Edward Fortescue, Viscount Eskdale, and a widower. He is also known as the Fallen Angel of Mayfair.

Heroine:

Harriet Hurst, the younger sister of the late Baron Huxley, friend of Edward Fortescue. She was a bluestocking spinster.

Other Characters:

- Ambrose Crosley – He is the 5th Earl of Pendlewood, and is affectionately known as "Pen." He is Edward Fortescue's best friend.

- Cedric Shipley – Lord Shipley is husband to Joanna Shipley, best friend to Harriet Hurst.

- Joanna Shipley – Lady Shipley is Harriet Hurst's best friend.

- Lord Vaughn – He was a friend to Harriet Hurst's late parents.

- Lady Vaughn – She was a friend to Harriet Hurst's late parents.

- Hugh Varley – He is the heir to his father, Baron Danforth. He is a reprobate, and was a potential "sham" suitor for Harriet Hurst's hand.

- William Thornton – He is the 5th Earl of Bardsea, and was the former brother-in-law of Edward Fortescue.

- Charles Frances Fortescue – He is the firstborn twin and heir of his parents, Edward and Harriet Hurst Fortescue.

- Sophia Elizabeth Fortescue – She is the younger twin of her brother, and is the second child of her parents, Edward and Harriet Hurst Fortescue.

Cast in the Lyon's Den:

- Bessie Dove-Lyon – She is the Black Widow of Whitehall, and the proprietor of the Lyon's Den.

LYON IN THE ROUGH

By Meara Platt

Book #22

Date: August 1817

Proud Scottish brothers, Cheyne, Matthew, and Lucas are known as the Lyons of Mar. Cheyne and Matthew have fallen in love and married their brides, will Lucas be next?

Lucas Lyon thought he could escape the matchmaking schemes of his distant relation, Bessie Dove-Lyon, by waiting for the morning of his departure from London to visit her. But she is ready for him, and he leaves her Lyon's Den to return to Edinburgh not only with the beautiful Beatrix MacGlory in tow, but her overly perfumed aunt and her aunt's little yipping dog.

Will he survive the ten-day journey in a cramped carriage with those three? More important, will he keep his hands off Beatrix? He is falling in love with her, but she is returning to Edinburgh for an arranged betrothal to another man. Since when has that stopped Lucas from claiming what he wants?

<u>Meet Lucas' brothers:</u>

Cheyne Lyon – The Lyon's Surprise

Matthew Lyon – Kiss of the Lyon

Hero:

Lucas Lyon, from the Lyon of Mar family, and a banker with the Royal Bank of Scotland

Heroine:

Beatrix MacGlory, daughter of Lord MacGlory

Other Characters:

- Lord MacGlory – He's the father of Beatrix MacGlory. He is also the head of the Royal Bank of Scotland.

- Lottie MacGlory – She's a cousin of Jocelyn MacGlory, Beatrix's late mother, and to Harriet Rochester. She is also Beatrix's stepmother.

- Harriet Rochester – Lady Rochester is the sister of Jocelyn MacGlory, Beatrix's mother, and had raised Beatrix after Jocelyn died.

- Abel Colquehoun – He's the Marquess of Greenock, and was Lord MacGlory's favored suitor for his daughter, Beatrix.

- Sally MacRaine – She is a wealthy woolen heiress, and was a friend to Beatrix MacGlory.

- Marjorie Cunningham – Lady Cunningham pursued Lucas Lyon in hopes of becoming his wife.

- Cheyne Lyon – He's the Duke of Mar, and is the hero of THE LYON'S SURPRISE.

- Jenny Lyon – She's the Duchess of Mar, and is the heroine of THE LYON'S SURPRISE.

- Fionn Lyon – He's the eldest son and heir of Cheyne and Jenny Lyon.

- Matthew Lyon – He's a mathematician and is the hero of KISS OF THE LYON.

- Danielle Lyon – She's the wife of Matthew Lyon, and is the heroine of KISS OF THE LYON.

Cast in the Lyon's Den:

- Bessie Dove-Lyon – She is the Black Widow of Whitehall, and the proprietor of the Lyon's Den. In this story, Lucas Lyon's granduncle was Sandstrom Lyon. They are related.

LADY LUCK AND THE LYON

By Chasity Bowlin

Book #23

Date: (None Given)

Kissing her had been a terrible miscalculation on his part. But laughing with her, finding something to enjoy about being in her company, that could well be an unmitigated disaster.

Garrick Bancroft, Viscount Lynley, is in dire need of both a wife and a fortune. He thought he'd found the perfect woman to fulfill both very nicely. But just days before they were to marry, she fled to Scotland in the arms of her younger brother's tutor. Left high and dry, there's only one option—Mrs. Bessie Dove-Lyon, London's most notorious matchmaker. With desperation as his constant companion, Garrick informs her that any young lady will do…so long as she has the appropriate accompanying fortune.

Miss Ellis Lockhart is in a terrible situation. Embarking on her fourth season with not a prospect in sight, her sisters are beginning to turn on her. Her infamously tightfisted father has refused to have more than one daughter launched in society at any given time. Until she makes a match, her sisters must hover in the background—waiting as spinsterhood looms over them all. Out of desperation, she reaches out to Mrs. Dove-Lyon and begs for her assistance…anyone will do, so long as he is a gentleman of rank.

There's really only one problem and it becomes apparent when the duo meet at the church for their wedding—Garrick and Ellis are not unknown to one another. In fact, they rather hate one another. But with the help of a little luck, and the meddling of Mrs. Dove-Lyon, they might soon realize that the line between love and hate is a fine one, and a fiery one, indeed.

Hero:

Garrick Bancroft, Viscount Lynley

Heroine:

Ellis Lockhart, the daughter of Winston Lockhart

Cast of Characters:

- Parker Lockhart – She's the younger sister of Ellis Lockhart.
- Leighton Lockhart – She's the younger sister of Ellis Lockhart.
- Merritt Lockhart – She's the younger sister of Ellis Lockhart.
- Winston Lockhart – He's the father of Ellis, Parker, Leighton, and Merritt Lockhart.
- Marianne Lockhart – She's the mother of Ellis, Parker, Leighton, and Merritt Lockhart. She was also hidden away in an asylum by her husband, Winston Lockhart.
- Eugenie Stonehurst – She's the aunt of Ellis, Parker, Leighton, and Merritt Lockhart.
- Philip Dorchester – He's a cousin to Garrick Bancroft.
- Madeline Keyes Easton – She's the heroine of TAMED BY THE LYON, and is now the Countess of Foxmore.
- Beaumont "Beau" Ramsden – He' the Marquess of Hexhaven, and is a client of Bessie Dove-Lyon.
- Miss Acres – She was the former fiancé of Garrick Bancroft, and was kidnapped before her wedding to Garrick.

Cast in the Lyon's Den:

- Bessie Dove-Lyon – She is the Black Widow of Whitehall, and the proprietor of the Lyon's Den.

RESCUED BY THE LYON

By C.H. Admirand

Book #24

Date: (None Given)

Captain Colin Broadbank returns to London aboard the HMS Britannia, and receives the tragic news his elder brother, Viscount Moreland, has perished from a virulent fever, and the life-changing edict that he is expected to leave the life he loves serving in His Majesty's Royal Navy. He is swept up in Earl Moreland's dictate that he accept the title, marry immediately and live the life of a titled landlubber!

Unwilling to add to his grieving family's burden, he accepts the title, but refuses to let his father parade suitable brides in front of him. The last thing he wants is a simpering miss just out of the schoolroom without a thought of her own. At his younger brother's suggestion, he decides to try his luck, and find his own bride, at Mrs. Dove-Lyon's famed establishment—The Lyon's Den.

Miss Gemma Atherton's father is a wealthy Cit, with an eye on maintaining control of her considerable fortune after he marries her off to an older business contemporary, one who will agree to go into business with him for the next five years. He treats her like the bag of coin she begins to feel is all that recommends her.

When her father discovers Gemma's younger brother has not quit gambling, he threatens to send her brother to America. She cannot

"

bear for that to happen. Not a typical young miss, Gemma takes her future in her own hands. She sews a reticule large enough to conceal her grandfather's dueling pistol, hires a hack, and heads to The Lyon's Den. Her plan is to meet with Mrs. Dove-Lyon and persuade her to find a husband who will agree to pay off Gemma's brother's debt before he accepts Gemma's dowry. Convinced their future is in their own hands, the two are bent on a course of their own making—destined to collide in the midst of The Lyon's Den!

The Broadbank Family

Colin and Gemma in Rescued by the Lyon

Edmund and Addy in Captivated by the Lyon

Hero:

Colin Broadbank, the new Viscount Moreland

Heroine:

Gemma Atherton, the daughter of a wealthy Cit

Other Characters:

- Edmund Broadbank – He's the younger brother of Colin Broadbank.

- Adam Broadbank – He is the father of Colin and Edmund Broadbank, and is known as Earl Templeton.

- Mr. Atherton – He's a wealthy Cit, and is the father of Gemma Atherton.

- Gordon Coventry – He was a former captain and naval hero, and his wounds reveal he's missing an eye and has a lame arm. He is also the Duke of Wyndmere's London man-of-affairs.

- Gavin King – He is a Bow Street Runner, and works with Captain Coventry.

- Garahan – He is one of the Duke of Wyndmere's guards.

- Lord Harkwell – He was the potential suitor for Miss Atherton's hand, and was approved of by Gemma's father.

Cast in the Lyon's Den:

- Bessie Dove-Lyon – She is the Black Widow of Whitehall, and the proprietor of the Lyon's Den.
- Titan – He's the head of the wolf pack at the Lyon's Den. He has a maimed hand from his service in the military.
- Snug – He's one of the escorts at the Lyon's Den.

PRETTY LITTLE LYON

By Katherine Bone

Book #25

Date: 1814

If you do not marry by Season's end, I shall expose the seedy side of your father's past, thereby damaging his reputation—and yours by proxy—condemning you both to a life of destitution and despair.

Who is sending Charlotta Walcot threatening notes? Why would anyone cast aspersions against her father, a mild-mannered professor of antiquities at Cambridge University? As for herself, although she has no plans to wed, why would that be of issue to anyone to save herself? Desperate to swerve the scandal that would destroy both her and her father's reputations, Charlotta dares to venture into the Lyon's Den, a gambling hall and house of ill repute in London's fashionable White-hall. There, she begs its owner, the mysterious Black Widow, Mrs. Bessie Dove-Lyon, to use her connections to identify her blackmailer.

But that is not the end of Charlotta's troubles. Obliged to attend her cousins' coming-out ball, she collides with Lord Septimus Grey. After witnessing the delivery of another unpleasant note to her, Septimus offers his help. But how can Charlotta place her trust in him since he is the man who, years ago, stole her young and impressionable heart?

Hero:

Septimus Grey, a former student of Professor Walcot, and is now Baron Grey

Heroine:

Charlotta "Lottie" Walcot, daughter of Bertram Walcot and Bessie Dove Lyons

Other Characters:

- Bertram Walcot – He is a Cambridge professor, former teacher of Septimus Grey, and is the father of Charlotta Walcot.
- Everard Walcot – He is the older brother of Bertram Walcot, and is the 5th Viscount Steere.
- Mary Walcot – She's the wife of Everard Walcot, Viscountess Steere, and is the mother of Parthenia, Delphi, and Augusta.
- Parthenia Steere – She's the oldest child and daughter of Lord and Lady Steere.
- Delphi Steere – She is a twin daughter of Lord and Lady Steere.
- Augusta Steere – She is a twin daughter of Lord and Lady Steere.

Cast in the Lyon's Den:

- Bessie Dove-Lyon – She is the Black Widow of Whitehall, and the proprietor of the Lyon's Den. In this novel it is revealed that Bessie is the birth mother of Charlotta "Lottie" Walcot from her affair with Bertram Walcot.
- Titan – He's the head of the wolf pack at the Lyon's Den.
- Daniel Bates – He is the doorman at the Lyon's Den.

The Courage of a Lyon

By Linda Rae Sande

Book #26

Date: September 1815

Their earldom is at stake. Can they save their futures and find love along the way?

Recovering from his wartime injuries and returning home to an earldom on the brink of bankruptcy, Captain Charles Audley is faced with the momentous task of settling his mischievous brother's debts. But try as he might, he can't take his mind off the angel of a nurse who cared for him on the battlefield. And after he crosses paths with an enigmatic matchmaker with a strange proposition, it quickly becomes clear that he might not have seen the last of his wartime beauty.

Meanwhile, James heads to Cambridgeshire, dead-set on winning the hand – and the hefty dowry – of a marquess' daughter. But when he discovers her already taken, he finds his eye drawn to her rebellious and fiercely independent younger sister. James can't bear the thought of returning home empty-handed... and although Lady Eloise is convinced he's only interested in courting her sister, an attraction begins to bubble to the surface that leaves her questioning James' true intentions.

With their earldom at stake and two young women desperate for men who can understand their deepest desires, can Charles and James find real love? And will the cunning talents of matchmaker Mrs. Dove-Lyon come to the rescue?

Hero:

Charles Audley, Captain in the British army, and younger brother of the Earl of Leicester, James Audley

Heroine:

Amy Sinclair, nurse in the British army and daughter of Colonel and Mrs. Sinclair

Hero:

James Audley, Earl of Leicester, and eldest brother of Charles Audley.

Heroine:

Eloise "El" Wilson, youngest daughter of the Marquess and Marchioness of Huntsford.

Other Characters:

- Elias Sinclair – Colonel Sinclair died after the Battle of Waterloo. He is the father of Amy Sinclair, and the husband of Margaret Sinclair.
- Margaret Sinclair – She's the widow of Elias Sinclair, and the mother of Amy Sinclair.
- Major Culkins – He's a close friend of Colonel and Mrs. Sinclair, and is interested in Mrs. Sinclair after the passing of her husband.
- __________ Wilson – He's the Marquess of Huntsford, husband of Marguerite Wilson, and the father of Stephanie and Eloise Wilson.
- Marguerite Wilson – She's the Marchioness of Huntsford, and is the mother of Stephanie and Eloise Wilson.
- Stephanie Wilson – She's the eldest daughter of Lord and Lady Huntsford, and is the oldest sister of Eloise Wilson.

- Mark O'Riley – He was a corporal in the British army, and was the former valet of the late Colonel Sinclair. He later became the valet to Captain Charles Audley.

Cast in the Lyon's Den:

- Bessie Dove-Lyon – She is the Black Widow of Whitehall, and the proprietor of the Lyon's Den.

- Titan – He's the head of the wolf pack at the Lyon's Den. He also was at the Battle of Waterloo at the same time Captain Charles Audley and Colonel Sinclair was.

- Egeus – He's one of the wolf pack at the Lyon's Den.

PRIDE OF LYONS

By *Jenna Jaxon*

Book #27

Date: June 1818

What's a young lady to do when a powerful lord tries to abscond with her and make her his mistress? When you're Miss Honoria Quinn, you leap from his carriage and run like the wind to find some place to hide. Trouble is, Honoria mistakenly chooses The Lyon's Den, a disreputable gambling house as her sanctuary, a move that ends up with her having to make another choice at the hands of the Den's matchmaking proprietor Mrs. Dove-Lyons: wed a complete stranger or become the lord's mistress.

No good deed goes unpunished… Thomas, Lord Braeton agrees to attend a wager at The Lyon's Den only to keep his brother-in-law out of trouble. What he doesn't count on is becoming embroiled in one of Mrs. Dove-Lyons's schemes to marry him off. But when he tries to come to the aid of another peer, Thomas finds the only honorable thing he can do to save Miss Quinn's reputation is put aside his hopes for a love match for himself and instead offer to marry her.

Hero:

Thomas Braeton, a wealthy nobleman

Heroine:

Honoria Quinn, daughter of a vicar, and paid companion/caretaker for Mrs. Edwards

Other Characters:

- Geoffrey Longford – He's the best friend of Lord Braeton.
- Lord Rochdale – He's the brother-in-law of Lord Braeton.
- Joanna Rochdale – She's the sister of Thomas Braeton.
- Aeneas Quinn – He's a vicar, and is the father of Honoria Quinn.
- Anne Quinn – She's the mother of Honoria Quinn.
- Louis Danford – Lord Danford is the husband of Caroline Danford.
- Caroline Danford – Lady Danford is the wife of Lord Danford, and is the daughter of Mrs. Edwards.
- Mrs. Edwards – She's the mother of Caroline Danford.

Cast in the Lyon's Den:

- Bessie Dove-Lyon – She is the Black Widow of Whitehall, and the proprietor of the Lyon's Den.
- Demetrius – A guard at the Lyon's Den.

THE LYON'S SHARE

By Cerise DeLand

Book #28

Date: May 1815

She'd spend every last penny to marry again for security, comfort—or even friendship. He'd win her wager, possess her, keep her for himself—even if he'd never win her love.

Adriana, Lady Benton, has many regrets—and one hope. To wed a good man to gain a life to which she is entitled. One free of sorrow, penury and ridicule. Appealing to Mrs. Dove-Lyon, Adriana hopes to attract one man who may appreciate her assets. But never need her love.

Colonel Sidney Wolf, once hailed as the ruthless 'Hound of the Horse Guards', vows to end Adriana's hardships. He's home from the wars and faces the daunting task of filling his father's role as the Earl of Middlethorpe. Believing only Adriana will do as his helpmate, he strikes a deal with Dove-Lyon that brings him the one woman he admires. The one woman he tells himself he can live with—and never touch.

But the nearness of his funny, charming, beautiful bride drives him mad. Knowing she will never love other than her first husband, can he keep his hands—and his heart to himself? And if he doesn't, can she ever forgive him?

Hero:

Sidney Wolf, 6th Earl of Middlethorpe, and former childhood friend of Paul and Adriana Benton

Heroine:

Adriana Benton, formerly Baroness Benton from her first marriage to Baron Benton

Other Characters:

- Paul Benton – He was Baron Benton, and was the late husband of Adriana Benton. He was a captain in the British army and a war hero, who was injured during the war and was an invalid.

- Liza Crowden – She is the older sister of Adriana Benton, and is Lady Norbridge.

- Henry Crowden – He's Lord Norbridge, and is a friend to Sidney Wolf, and brother-in-law to Adriana Benton.

- Barbara Crowden – She's the daughter of Lord and Lady Norbridge, and the niece of Adriana Benton.

Cast in the Lyon's Den:

- Bessie Dove-Lyon – She is the Black Widow of Whitehall, and the proprietor of the Lyon's Den.

THE HEART OF A LYON

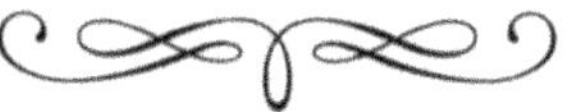

By Anna St. Claire

Book #29

Date: August 1815

She needs a miracle to save her, but he refuses to consider marriage, until a pretend betrothal changes how he sees her.

Riddled with guilt and haunted by nightmares over the tragic death of his father, Henry Stanton, the Earl of Egerton, returns home a broken man and seeks solace in the excesses of the Lyon's Den. He's sworn to never marry, but a chance meeting with the woman who captured his heart over a decade ago forces him to rethink his decision. Unwillingness to change his mind may prevent him from discovering what his heart and soul needs most.

Lady Olivia Dawson wants a love match, but her family's financial ruin upends her perfect life and worse, the vile man who holds her family's fortune demands her hand. When she meets the childhood friend she's never forgotten, she realizes he's everything she's wants.

A mother desperate to save her daughter's future appeals to the Black Widow of Whitehall who spins a web of hearts, high stakes bets, and intrigue—but the widow's plan places Olivia's life in the path of a killer. Henry and Olivia's futures will hang in the balance, unless they can find a way to trust one another with their lives and hearts.

Hero:

Henry Stanton, Earl of Egerton, and younger brother of the Duke of Kendall

Heroine:

Olivia Dawson, daughter of Lord and Lady Southwood

Other Characters:

- Lawrence Stanton – He's the late Duke of Kendall. He went to pick up his two sons from the battlefield when he perished after their ship was hit by mortar.
- Caroline Stanton – She's the dowager Duchess of Kendall. She's the mother of Albert, Henry, Lauren, and Roger.
- Albert Stanton – He's the current Duke of Kendall, and is the older brother of Henry, Lauren, and Roger Stanton.
- Roger Stanton – He's the younger adopted brother of Henry, Albert, and Lauren Stanton. He was an orphan until the Duke and Duchess of Kendall adopted him.
- Lauren Stanton – She's the younger sister of Albert, Henry, and Roger Stanton.
- Simon Dawson – He's the Earl of Southwood, and is the father of Olivia Dawson.
- Phoebe Dawson – She's the Countess of Southwood, and is the mother of Olivia Dawson.
- Dillon Langdon – He's a viscount, and is a card cheat. He was planning on being a suitor for Lady Olivia's hand.
- Victoria Crinoline – She's the mistress of Lord Langdon, and is also an actress.
- John Ford – He is a Bow Street Runner, hired to help solve the attempted murder of Albert Stanton, Duke of Kendall.
- Michael Foxx – He is a Bow Street Runner, hired to help solve the attempted murder of Albert Stanton, Duke of Kendall.

- Mr. Wren – He is a Bow Street Runner, hired to help solve the attempted murder of Albert Stanton, Duke of Kendall.

Cast in the Lyon's Den:

- Bessie Dove-Lyon – She is the Black Widow of Whitehall, and the proprietor of the Lyon's Den.
- Philostrate – He is a footman at the Lyon's Den.
- Helene – Also known as Mrs. Crutch, she is a servant and go-between for Mrs. Bessie Dove-Lyon at the Lyon's Den.

INTO THE LYON OF FIRE

By Abigail Bridges

Book #30

Date: July 1814

Being indebted to the Black Widow of Whitehall could be a catastrophe in the making—or a path to salvation.

Sarah Montague Ainsworth has tucked away the darkest of her secrets. A widow who never wants to marry again, Sarah is relieved her abusive husband died but is struggling to keep her household solvent. She bought her current home with a loan from Mrs. Dove-Lyon, owner of the infamous Lyon's Den, and makes her payments by gambling on the ladies' side of the notorious hell. Sarah also never plans show her face again in Society—for good reason. One of her husband's last acts was to shove her into a fireplace. Sarah survived but is scarred over the right side of her body—including her face. The Lyon's Den—and a black veil—are the perfect places to hide.

Matthew Rydell, the newly invested Duke of Embleton, is in a hurry. A colonel under Wellington, Matthew has been at war—and prefers his life in that arena. But his father's unexpected death changed all that. Back in England to settle the estate and accept his rank, he acquiesces to his mother's insistence that he marry before returning Wellington's side. With no patience for Society balls and soirees, he turns to the Lyon's Den for help.

When Matthew proposes a sum Mrs. Dove-Lyon cannot resist—and chooses Sarah as his potential mate—the proprietor of the Lyon's Den calls in Sarah's loan. Desperate, Sarah agrees to marry the duke—only to discover she is not the only one hiding dark secrets.

Hero:

Matthew Rydell, newly invested Duke of Embleton, and in service to the Duke of Wellington in the army

Heroine:

Sarah Ainsworth, the widow of the late Lord Crewood

Other Characters:

- Phyllida Rydell – She's the dowager Duchess of Embleton, and is the mother of Matthew Rydell, the current Duke of Embleton. She also has eight other sons and one daughter.
- Mark Rydell – He's the second oldest son of Phyllida Rydell, and is a brother to Matthew Rydell.
- Paul Rydell – He is a younger son of Phyllida Rydell.
- Peter Rydell – He is a younger son of Phyllida Rydell.
- James Rydell – He is a younger son of Phyllida Rydell.
- Theophilus Rydell – He s a younger son of Phyllida Rydell.
- Timothy Rydell – He is a younger son of Phyllida Rydell.
- Robert Rydell – He is the oldest son and heir of Matthew and Sarah Rydell, the current Duke and Duchess of Embleton.
- ________ Ainsworth – He's the current Lord Crewood, after the passing of Sarah Ainsworth late husband.
- ________ Ainsworth – She's the current Lady Crewood, after her husband inherits the earldom after the previous Lord Crewood passed away.
- Hiram Lewis – He is a Bow Street Runner.

Cast in the Lyon's Den:

- Bessie Dove-Lyon – She is the Black Widow of Whitehall, and the proprietor of the Lyon's Den.

- Helene – She is a servant at the Lyon's Den.

LYON OF THE HIGHLANDS

By Emily Royal

Book #31

Date: 1818

Marriage to an Earl destroyed her—can a highland beast mend her heart? After surviving an abusive marriage to an older man, Wilhelmina Redstone retreated from society. Her stepson's wife, Lily, once her rival, promises to find Mina the perfect husband—a man to love her as she deserves—by engaging the services of Bessie Dove-Lyon, proprietress of the Lyon's Den, who secured Lily's own marriage. On entering the Lyon's Den, Mina glimpses a huge, savage Highlander among the dandies, and his appearance both terrifies and thrills her.

Laird Duncan MacLeish must marry for money—quickly—to avoid bankruptcy. Resigning himself to a loveless match, he sets off for London, and the infamous Lyon's Den, where wealthy harridans are rumored to do, and pay, anything to wed a title. But, when he competes in an extraordinary game, he learns that the prospective bride is no harridan, but a widow with soulful eyes and a tragic past.

Carried off to the Highlands, a world away from the genteel society she's always known, Mina begins to fall for the stranger she's married—a man whose savage appearance belies his tender heart, and whose body ignites previously unknown sensations. But, if Mina is to find the happiness she craves, she must first conquer the nightmares of her past.

<u>The Redstone Family</u>

Lily and Mason in A Lyon's Pride

Mina and Duncan in Lyon of the Highlands

Hero:

Duncan MacLeish, Laird of Kilduggan Castle

Heroine:

Wilhelmina "Mina" Redstone, widow of the late Earl of Redstone

Other Characters:

- Mason Redstone – He is the hero of A LYON'S PRIDE, and is the 11th Earl of Redstone. He is also the stepson of Mina Redstone. He has three children in this novel.

- Lily Redstone – She's the heroine of A LYON'S PRIDE, the current Countess of Redstone, and is the mother of three children.

- Francesca de Viliers – She's the widow of a baronet, and is the mother of Lily Redmond. She also was "La Flamme," a famous courtesan at the Lyon's Den.

- Amelia Diamond – She's the twin daughter of Mason and Lily Redstone.

- Belinda Diamond – She's the twin daughter of Mason and Lily Redstone.

- Francesco Redstone – He is the young son and heir of Mason and Lily Redstone.

- Fraser – He is the Duke of Molineux, and is a friend of Duncan MacLeish.

- Simon Dewar – He is Viscount Lowry, and was hoping to be a suitor for Mina's hand in marriage.

- Callum MacLeish – He is the younger brother of Duncan MacLeish.

- Flora MacLeish – She is the wife of Callum MacLeish.

- Jamie MacLeish – He is a son of Callum and Flora MacLeish.
- Shona MacLeish – She is the daughter of Callum and Flora MacLeish.
- Hamish MacLeish – He is the son and heir of Duncan and Mina MacLeish.

Cast in the Lyon's Den:

- Bessie Dove-Lyon – She is the Black Widow of Whitehall, and the proprietor of the Lyon's Den.
- Hermia – She is a servant at the Lyon's Den.

THE LYON'S PUZZLE

By Sandra Sookoo

Book #32

Date: October 1817

A dark and tortured soul… Montague Bassage—12th Earl of Pennington—wants nothing to do with romance or anything else, frankly. After the fickle threads of fate took his two fiancées, he retreated within himself. Over the years, he's made himself into the worst man in London—a true beast. A rake to be sure. In his cups more often than not. Skilled at wagering, absolutely. Most of his time is spent at the Lyon's Den gaming hell, where his only joy is winning at the tables.

Besieged by rumor and innuendo… Mrs. Adriana Roberts nee Stapleton, eldest daughter of Baron Kentwood, is a widow accused of killing her reprobate husband. In the scandal that followed his death, she returned home, only to dance attendance on her much younger and more beautiful sister, for the chit still has a chance of a good match. But when that sister's hand is lost at a card table to the Worst Man in London, she has to do something.

The past has a habit of retaining a grip… When the owner of the Lyon's Den arranges a devious marriage between them, they have no choice but to comply. As Montague acts like an enraged beast, Adriana vows to keep the union as a marriage of convenience despite the intense attraction present. But when understanding chips away at their defenses, romance might have a chance if they choose to trust after years of disappointment and hurt instead of locking themselves away into darkness. ***Or else Mrs. Dove-Lyon will make certain they get exactly what they want…***

Hero:

Montague Bassage, the 12th Earl of Pennington, and dubbed the "worst man in London"

Heroine:

Adriana Stapleton Roberts, the widow of a merchant, and daughter of Baron Kentwood

Other Characters:

- Thomas – He is Viscount Ashbury, and is the best friend of Montague Bassage.
- _______ Stapleton – He is Baron Kentwood, and is the father of Adriana Stapleton and Sybil Stapleton.
- _______ Stapleton – She is Baroness Kentwood, and is the mother of Adriana Stapleton and Sybil Stapleton.
- Sybil Stapleton – She is the daughter of Baron and Baroness Kentwood, and is the sister of Adriana Stapleton.
- Richard Somerford – He is the younger son of a viscount, and is a suitor for Adriana Stapleton's hand in marriage.

Cast in the Lyon's Den:

- Bessie Dove-Lyon – She is the Black Widow of Whitehall, and the proprietor of the Lyon's Den.
- Helena – She's a servant in the Lyon's Den.
- Mr. Vance – He's the high-ranking representative overseeing the card tables at the Lyon's Den.

Lyon at the Altar

By Lily Harlem

Book #33

Date: (None Given)

Miss Anna Toussaint's first love is passionate, addictive and forbidden and leaves deep scars on her heart that can never be healed—or can they? With a scandal in her past, a dark smear of shame, Miss Anna Toussaint finds herself in dire need of a husband and under the rather dubious wing of The Black Widow of Whitehall.

The Black Widow works in unconventional ways that only she understands and during an evening of twists and turns, intrigue and suspense Anna finds herself betrothed to a mysterious masked gentleman. At the altar a flick of a wrist sees his devilish mask removed and reveals the wickedly handsome viscount who'd allowed her to fall to rack and ruin at the same time as shattering her heart and soul.

And now she is his wife! Until death parts them! The entire situation is preposterous, shocking, unbelievable, except now she must take on the roles of Viscountess De-Wold and his lover. Can a marriage that starts on the rocks ever rise above the waves? And can feelings long buried be allowed to burn brightly again?

Hero:

Frank Webb, current Viscount De-Wold

Heroine:

Anna Toussaint, daughter of Frank Webb's former French tutor

Cast of Characters:

- Emily Toussaint – She was the former French tutor to Frank Webb, and is the mother of Anna Toussaint.
- James Webb – He is the late father of Frank Webb, and was the previous viscount.
- Bertha Webb – She is the widow of James Webb, and is the dowager Viscountess De-Wold.
- Gerard – He's the Duke of Hillcrest, and is the best friend of Frank Webb.

Cast in the Lyon's Den:

- Bessie Dove-Lyon – She is the Black Widow of Whitehall, and the proprietor of the Lyon's Den.
- Helena – She's a servant in the Lyon's Den.
- Hermia – She's a servant in the Lyon's Den.
- Titan – He's the head of the wolf pack in the Lyon's Den.
- Theseus – He is a bouncer at the Lyon's Den.
- Egeus – He is a bouncer in the Lyon's Den.

CAPTIVATED BY THE LYON

By C.H. Admirand

Book #34

Date: (None Given)

A man searching for the truth, and a woman afraid to reveal it, cross paths in the middle of the notorious Lyon's Den! A year after his brother Adam, the former Viscount Moreland's untimely death, Edmund Broadbank is still searching for clues to unravel the identity of the mysterious woman who arrived at Templeton House the day after his brother died.

Adelaide Fernside assumes the role of mother to her younger sister when their parents die in a tragic accident. Her sister craves being the center of attention and succumbs to the lure of the stage, only to return home when she becomes pregnant.

Unable to resist the glitter of her former life, Lily leaves her babe behind. Addy had not planned on assuming the care of her infant nephew but becomes mother to her sister's child. When word reaches her that someone has been asking questions about Adam in the village, she realizes she needs the protection of a husband. In a bold move, she dons the guise of a widow and travels to London with Adam, to seek the aid of Mrs. Dove-Lyon in finding a husband. Her nephew deserves to have a father, even if Addy never planned to marry.

Elated to receive word the woman rumored to have had a liaison with his brother Adam has been seen entering the Lyon's Den,

"

Edmund Broadbank pays a visit to Mrs. Dove-Lyon. Neither Addy, nor Edmund realize that Mrs. Dove-Lyon has hatched a plan of her own— to match the two of them!

<u>The Broadbank Family</u>

Colin and Gemma in Rescued by the Lyon

Edmund and Addy in Captivated by the Lyon

Hero:

Edmund Broadbank, Sr., the younger brother of Colin Broadbank, Viscount Moreland

Heroine:

Adelaide "Addy" Fernside, the older sister of actress Lily Lovecote

Other Characters:

- Edmund Broadbank, Jr. – He's the firstborn son and heir of Edmund Broadbank, Sr., and his wife, Addy Fernside Broadbank.

- Adam Broadbank, III – He's the young son of Adam Broadbank, Jr., and Lily Lovecote, and is being raised by Addy Fernside; his aunt.

- Lily Lovecote – She's the younger sister of Addy Fernside, and is an actress. She is the mother of Adam Broadbank, III, (son of the late Adam Broadbank, Jr.), who is being raised by her older sister.

- Colin Broadbank – He's the hero of RESCUED BY THE LYON, and is the new Viscount Moreland.

- Gemma Atherton – She's the heroine of RESCUED BY THE LYON, and is the daughter of the wealthy Mr. Atherton.

- Adam Broadbank, Sr. – He is the father of Colin and Edmund Broadbank, and is known as Earl Templeton.

- Gordon Coventry – He was a former captain and naval hero, and his wounds reveal he's missing an eye and has a lame arm. He is also the Duke of Wyndmere's London man-of-affairs.

- Gavin King – He is a Bow Street Runner, and works with Captain Coventry.
- Catherine "Kit" Huntington – She's a client of Mrs. Bessie Dove-Lyon, and is a new friend to Addy Fernside.
- Lord Honeywell – He is the disreputable suitor of Lily Lovecote.

Cast in the Lyon's Den:
- Bessie Dove-Lyon – She is the Black Widow of Whitehall, and the proprietor of the Lyon's Den.
- Titan – He's the head of the wolf pack at the Lyon's Den. He has a maimed hand from his service in the military.
- Snug – He's one of the escorts at the Lyon's Den.
- Hermia – She's a woman's door attendant at the Lyon's Den.
- Helena – She's a woman's door attendant at the Lyon's Den.

THE LYON'S SECRET

By Laura Trentham

Book #35

Date: (None Given)

Vicars make the best spies...But should vicars be this sexy and dangerous? When Mr. Josiah Barrymore is summoned by the Black Widow of Whitehall, he can't contain his curiosity—and trepidation. After all, Mrs. Dove-Lyon is the owner of a notorious gaming hell in London, and he is a vicar, albeit one with a secret. When she produces the sister of his dead best friend, he is shocked. What is Amelia doing in a notorious gaming hell? And when did she grow into such a beautiful woman?

In desperation, Miss Amelia Fielding arrives on Mrs. Dove-Lyon doorstep seeking help. What she receives is unexpected. When a mutually beneficial marriage is proposed between Amelia and Josiah by Mrs. Dove-Lyon, Amelia is torn. She needs the protection he can provide, but doesn't want to be in his power. Or does she? Her time at the Lyon's Den has opened her eyes, and the pull she feels toward Josiah is no longer the simple tendresse of a young girl, but the desire of a woman.

Josiah owes it to his best friend to protect Amelia, but that's not the only reason he submits to marriage. He can't deny the blistering attraction he feels toward Amelia even if bringing a wife into his secret life will prove dangerous to them both.

Hero:

Josiah Barrymore, currently a vicar, and also in service to the Crown working as a spy for the Home Office

Heroine:

Amelia Fielding, younger sister of Josiah Barrymore's deceased best friend

Other Characters:

- James Fielding – He's the older brother of Amelia Fielding, and is a wastrel.

- Gray Masterson – Josiah works for Sir Gray at the Home Office.

- _________ Drinkwater – Mrs. Drinkwater is the cook and the housekeeper at the vicarage where Josiah and Amelia live at. She also helps with any spy business that Josiah Barrymore needs help with.

- _________ Hanson – Mr. Hanson is a traitorous spy.

- Grace Hamilton – She's Amelia Barrymore's best friend in the parish of Upper Wexham.

- Bess _________ – She is a young pre-teen orphan sent by Mrs. Dove-Lyon to live with Josiah and Amelia Barrymore in Upper Wexham.

Cast in the Lyon's Den:

- Bessie Dove-Lyon – She is the Black Widow of Whitehall, and the proprietor of the Lyon's Den. She was also a very close friend of Mrs. Fielding when they were children. Mrs. Fielding is Amelia's late mother.

THE TALONS OF THE LYON

By Jude Knight

Book #36

Date: April 1817

Lance Versey owes Mrs. Dove Lyon a promise. Fulfilling it will cost him the life he enjoys and win him the life he wants.

The death of Lady Frogmore's neglectful and disloyal husband should have been a relief. But then her nasty brother-in-law seizes her three children and turns her out, telling the whole of Society that she is a crude, vulgar, and loose woman. Without allies or friends, Serafina, Lady Frogmore, turns to Mrs. Dove Lyon, also known as the Black Widow of Whitehall for help, paying her by promising to perform an unspecified favor at a time of the Mrs. Dove Lyon's choice.

Lord Lancelot Versey has always tried to be a perfect gentleman, and a gentleman honors his debts, even when an unwise wager obliges him to escort a notorious widow into Society. But Lady Frogmore is not what he expects, and helping her becomes a quest worthy of the knight for whom he was named. Except Mrs. Dove Lyon calls in Seraphina's promise. The favor she asks might destroy all they have found together.

Hero:

Lancelot "Lance" Versey, younger brother of the Duke of Dellborough

Heroine:

Seraphina Frogmore, widow of the late Baron Frogmore

Other Characters:

- Percy Versey – He's the Duke of Dellborough, and is the older brother of Lance Versey.

- Aurelia Versey – She's the Duchess of Dellborough, and is the sister-in-law of Lance Versey. She's also the estranged aunt of Moriah Henshaw.

- Barbara Devereaux – She's the eldest daughter of the Duke and Duchess of Dellborough, and is married to Lord Devereaux.

- Elaine Versey Barker – She's the younger sister of Percy Versey and Lance Versey, and is married to Lord Barker.

- _______ Barker – Viscount Barker is married to Viscountess Elaine Versey Barker, the sister of Lance and Percy.

- Jenna Versey – She's a countess, and is married to the Percy's eldest son and heir.

- Isolde _______ – She's Lance and Percy's younger sister, and is now a countess.

- Nineve _______ – She's Lance and Percy's younger sister, and is married to a commoner, who works for the government.

- Marcus Frogmore – He is Seraphina's brother-in-law.

- Virginia Frogmore – She's married to Marcus Frogmore, and is Seraphina's sister-in-law.

- Hannah Frogmore – She's the eldest daughter of the late Henry Frogmore, and his wife, Seraphina Frogmore.

- Helena Frogmore – She's the second child of the late Henry Frogmore, and his wife, Seraphina Frogmore.

- Harry Frogmore – He is the youngest son of the late Henry Frogmore, and his wife, Seraphina Frogmore. He is also the current Baron Frogmore, as his father, the previous baron, passed away.

- Evelyn Worthington – She is Lord Barker's pious aunt.
- _________ Haverford – The Duke of Haverford is a friend of the Versey family.
- _________ Haverford – The Duchess of Haverford is a friend of the Versey family.
- Vincent St. John – He is the hero of TO CLAIM A LYON'S HEART. The Earl of Saxton is also the best friend of Lance Versey, and is courting Moriah Henshaw, the estranged niece of Aurelia Versey, Duchess Dellborough.
- Moriah Henshaw – She is the heroine of TO CLAIM A LYON'S HEART. She is also the best friend of Seraphina Frogmore, and is a widow on the outskirts of polite society. She is the estranged niece of Aurelia Versey, Duchess Dellborough.

Cast in the Lyon's Den:

- Bessie Dove-Lyon – She is the Black Widow of Whitehall, and the proprietor of the Lyon's Den.

THE LYON AND THE LAMB

By Elizabeth Keysian

Book #37

Date: (None Given)

He's dashed all her hopes. She won't ask him for help again. Only the production of an heir can save Lady Araminta Lamb. The problem is that she's a childless widow who, after an abusive marriage, can't bear the thought of a man's touch. But when her desperate attempt to adopt a child is foiled by the powerful Leo Chetwynd, Earl of Aylsham, there's only one option left to keep her home and her fragile sister safe. She must gamble everything on Mrs. Dove-Lyon's outrageous matchmaking scheme.

Playing by Society's rules hasn't done him any favors. Perhaps it's time to break those rules.

Leo Chetwynd needs money urgently or his precious orphans will be cast out. A disastrous business venture has cost him all his capital, and there's nothing left to offer but himself. Marriage to an heiress is the only solution that he and his scapegrace brother can think of, but first, he must go to the Lyon's Den and prove his skills as a lover. If Leo accepts Mrs. Dove-Lyon's choice of heiress, sight unseen, the orphanage and the family name will be saved. He can only pray that the chosen heiress isn't the anonymous veiled widow who has become his enemy. She's the last woman on earth he could ever marry.

Hero:

Leo Chetwynd, Earl of Aylsham, and Principal Trustee of Lady Aylsham's Foundling Hospital

Heroine:

Araminta Lamb, widow of the late Horatio Lamb

Other Characters:

- Belinda Bellamy – She's the younger sister of Araminta Lamb, and suffers from melancholia.
- Roland Chetwynd – He's the younger charming ne'er do-well younger brother of Leo Chetwynd.

Cast in the Lyon's Den:

- Bessie Dove-Lyon – She is the Black Widow of Whitehall, and the proprietor of the Lyon's Den.
- Titan – He's the head wolf at the Lyon's Den.
- Hermia – She's a woman's escort at the Lyon's Den.
- Petrushka – She's the gilded acrobat performer at the Lyon's Den.

TO CLAIM A LYON'S HEART

By Sherry Ewing

Book #38

Date: April 1817

A gambler's bet. A widow's burden. Will one game of chance change their lives?

Vincent St. John, Marquis of Saxton, knows full well his duties to the duchy. His responsibilities have been drilled into him since his birth. He has no chance of finding a bride who will see him for who he truly is; they only see the title, not the man. A bet with Mrs. Dove-Lyon, the Black Widow of Whitehall, is just a diversion. Losing may win him everything.

Mrs. Moriah Henshaw has known her fair share of despair. The death of her parents and later her husband left her destitute with no option but to become a man's mistress. Years later, her tarnished reputation outweighs her excellent birth, and keeps her from being accepted back into society. When her friend pays an outrageous sum to Mrs. Dove-Lyon to find Moriah a husband, Moriah cannot believe she will win anything.

When Vincent meets Moriah, he becomes determined to return her to her rightful place in society. But one accident after another threatens Moriah's life, and neither of them will win in the game of love unless he can find out who is out to harm her.

Hero:

Vincent St. John, the Marquis of Saxton, and current heir to his father's dukedom

Heroine:

Moriah Henshaw, the estranged granddaughter of the Earl of Harrowby, and is a widow living on the outskirts of polite society

Other Characters:

- Roger __________ – He's the Earl of Harrowby, and is the estranged grandfather of Moriah Henshaw.
- Aurelia Versey – She's the Duchess of Dellborough, and is Moriah's aunt.
- Percy Versey – He's married to Aurelia Versey, and is the Duke of Dellborough.
- Lance Versey – He's the younger brother of Percy Versey, and is the hero of THE TALONS OF THE LYON.
- Seraphina Versey – She's the wife of Lance Versey, and is the heroine of THE TALONS OF THE LYON.
- Charles St. John – He's the father of Vincent St. John is currently a duke.
- Rachel St. John – She's the mother of Vincent St. John and is currently a duchess.
- __________ – She's the Duchess of Winshire, and was previously the Duchess of Haverford. When her husband, the late Duke of Haverford passed away, she married the Duke of Winshire.
- __________ – He's the Duke of Haverford, and is the son and heir of the late Duke of Haverford, and the Duchess of Winshire (previously the Duchess of Haverford).
- Grace Lacey – She is married to Nicholas Lacey, and is a friend of Moriah Henshaw.

- Nicholas Lacey – Lord Lacey is married to Grace Lacey, and is a friend of Moriah Henshaw.
- Evelyn Worthington – She's the pious aunt of Lord Barker.
- Adam Page – He's the son of Matthew Page, who was the best friend of Roger, the Earl of Harrowby (Moriah's estranged grandfather). He's also the former lover of Moriah Henshaw, and is now the lover of Vincent St. John's previous mistress, Regina Patterson.
- Regina Patterson – She's the former mistress of Vincent St. John, and later becomes the mistress of Adan Page.
- Cassandra Vaughn – She is a friend of Moriah's, and is the leader of the Wicked Widow's Club.
- Patricia Moore – She is a friend of Moriah's, and is a member of the Wicked Widow's Club.
- Josephine Bouchard – She's a friend of Moriah's, and is a member of the Wicked Widow's Club.
- Asher Tyler – He is a friend of Vincent St. John, and is the Earl of Rowley.
- Lucius _______ – He is a friend of Vincent St. John, and is the Earl of Blackthorn.
- Gyles Hawley – He is a friend of Vincent St. John, and is the Marquis of Wickes.

Cast in the Lyon's Den:
- Bessie Dove-Lyon – She is the Black Widow of Whitehall, and the proprietor of the Lyon's Den.
- Hermia – She's a woman's escort at the Lyon's Den.
- Helena – She's a woman's escort at the Lyon's Den.
- Oberon – She's a female card dealer at the Lyon's Den.
- Snug – He's a guard at the Lyon's Den.
- Puck – He's a guard at the Lyon's Den.

Books Chronologically BY YEAR

This is a list of every novel and the year it is set in. This list is for all families, all novels, and is not grouped by families. It is grouped by year. Since some people like to read books chronologically by the year they are set in, regardless of family groups or series, this will be helpful to see where each book is set.

Book Title	Year Book Took Place	Author
Into the Lyon's Den	(None)	Jade Lee
Lyon Hearted	(None)	Jade Lee
Fed to the Lyon	(None)	Mary Lancaster
The Lyon's Laird	(None)	Hildie McQueen
The Lyon Sleeps Tonight	(None)	Elizabeth Ellen Carter
Always the Lyon Tamer	(None)	Emily E K Murdoch
How to Steal a Lyon's Fortune	(None)	Alanna Lucas
Lady Luck and the Lyon	(None)	Chasity Bowlin
Rescued by the Lyon	(None)	C.H. Admirand
Captivated by the Lyon	(None)	C.H. Admirand
Lyon at the Altar	(None)	Lily Harlem
The Lyon's Secret	(None)	Laura Trentham

The Lyon and the Lamb	(None)	Elizabeth Keysian
A Lyon in Her Bed	1814	Amanda Mariel
Pretty Little Lyon	1814	Katherine Bone
Fall of the Lyon	February 1814	Chasity Bowlin
The Scandalous Lyon	March 1814	Maggi Andersen
Tamed by the Lyon	March 1814	Chasity Bowlin
Into the Lyon of Fire	July 1814	Abigail Bridges
The Lyon's Den in Winter	December 1814	Whitney Blake
To Tame the Lyon	1815	Sky Purington
Lyon Eyes	February 1815	Lynne Connolly
The Lyon's Share	May 1815	Cerise DeLand
The Heart of a Lyon	August 1815	Anna St. Claire
The Courage of a Lyon	September 1815	Linda Rae Sande
Loved by the Lyon	March 1816	Collette Cameron
A Lyon's Pride	March 1816	Emily Royal
The Lyon's Lady Love	April 1816	Alexa Aston
The Lyon's Surprise	August 1816	Meara Platt
The Devilish Lyon	September 1816	Charlotte Wren
The Lyon's Prey	December 1816	Anna St. Clair
The Talons of the Lyon	April 1817	Jude Knight
To Claim a Lyon's Heart	April 1817	Sherry Ewing
Kiss of the Lyon	May 1817	Meara Platt
Lyon in the Rough	August 1817	Meara Platt
The Lyon's Puzzle	October 1817	Sandra Sookoo
Lyon of the Highlands	1818	Emily Royal
Pride of Lyons	June 1818	Jenna Jaxon

All Novels in Publication Order

1. INTO THE LYON'S DEN – Jade Lee

2. THE SCANDALOUS LYON – Maggi Andersen

3. FED TO THE LYON – Mary Lancaster

4. THE LYON'S LADY LOVE – Alexa Aston

5. THE LYON'S LAIRD – Hildie McQueen

6. THE LYON SLEEPS TONIGHT – Elizabeth Ellen Carter

7. A LYON IN HER BED – Amanda Mariel

8. FALL OF THE LYON – Chasity Bowlin

9. LYON'S PREY – Anna St. Clair

10. LOVED BY THE LYON – Collette Cameron

11. THE LYON'S DEN IN WINTER – Whitney Blake

12. KISS OF THE LYON – Meara Platt

13. ALWAYS THE LYON TAMER – Emily E K Murdoch

14. TO TAME THE LYON – Sky Purington

15. HOW TO STEAL A LYON'S FORTUNE – Alanna Lucas

16. THE LYON'S SURPRISE – Meara Platt

17. A LYON'S PRIDE – Emily Royal

18. LYON EYES – Lynne Connolly

19. TAMED BY THE LYON – Chasity Bowlin

20. LYON HEARTED – Jade Lee

21. THE DEVILISH LYON – Charlotte Wren

22. LYON IN THE ROUGH – Meara Platt

23. LADY LUCK AND THE LYON – Chasity Bowlin

24. RESCUED BY THE LYON – C.H. Admirand
25. PRETTY LITTLE LYON – Katherine Bone
26. THE COURAGE OF A LYON – Linda Rae Sande
27. PRIDE OF LYONS – Jenna Jaxon
28. THE LYON'S SHARE – Cerise DeLand
29. THE HEART OF A LYON – Anna St. Claire
30. INTO THE LYON OF FIRE – Abigail Bridges
31. LYON OF THE HIGHLANDS – Emily Royal
32. THE LYON'S PUZZLE – Sandra Sookoo
33. LYON AT THE ALTAR – Lily Harlem
34. CAPTIVATED BY THE LYON – C.H. Admirand
35. THE LYON'S SECRET – Laura Trentham
36. THE TALONS OF THE LYON – Jude Knight
37. THE LYON AND THE LAMB – Elizabeth Keysian
38. TO CLAIM A LYON'S HEART – Sherry Ewing

Master List of Main & Secondary Characters

This is a list of all main and secondary characters from the Lyon's Den novels.
A reference guide only.
All Characters are copyrighted.

Acres, _________ – She's the former fiancé of Garrick Bancroft, and was kidnapped before she was able to marry him. She appears in LADY LUCK AND THE LYON.

Ainsworth, _________ – Lady Ainsworth is the current Countess of Crewood, after her husband inherited the title from his relative. He appears in INTO THE LYON OF FIRE.

Ainsworth, _________ – Lord Ainsworth is the current Earl of Crewood after inheriting the title from his relative, the late Earl of Crewood. He appears in INTO THE LYON OF FIRE.

Ainsworth, Mabel – She is the only child of the late Duke of Surrey, and his wife, the Duchess of Surrey. She appears in TO TAME THE LYON.

Anglesey, Christopher – He's the Earl of Banbury, and is a friend to Evan Prescott, Lord Clarendon. He appears in LYON'S PREY.

Angus, William "Bill" – He is the hero of FED TO THE LYON. He is the Earl of Garvie.

Angus, Diana Wade – She is the heroine of FED TO THE LYON, and is the daughter of Lord and Lady Wade. She was previously the lady-of-the-bedchamber to the Princess of Wales.

Ashbury, Thomas – He is Viscount Ashbury, and is the best friend of Montague Bassage. He appears in THE LYON'S PUZZLE.

Ashby, William – Sir William is the stepfather of Margaret Upshaw, and appears in FALL OF THE LYON.

Atherton, ___________ – Mr. Atherton is a wealthy Cit, and is the father of Gemma Atherton Broadbank. He appears in RESCUED BY THE LYON.

Audley, Amy Sinclair – She is one of the heroines in THE COURAGE OF A LYON, and is the daughter of Colonel and Marguerite Sinclair. She was a nurse in the British Army and had nursed Captain Charles Sinclair back to health and marries him in this story.

Audley, Charles – He is one of the heroes of THE COURAGE OF A LYON, and is a Captain in the British army. He is the younger brother of the Earl of Leicester, James Audley. He marries Amy Sinclair.

Audley, Eloise "El" Wilson – She is one of the heroines of THE COURAGE OF A LYON, and is The daughter of the Marquess and Marchioness of Huntsford. She marries James Audley, Earl of Leicester.

Audley, James – He is one of the heroes of THE COURAGE OF A LYON, and is the Earl of Leicester. He is the eldest brother of Captain Charles Audley. He marries Eloise "El" Wilson, daughter of the Marquess and Marchioness of Huntsford.

Bamber, Simon – He is the former betrothed of Lady Diana Wade, and appears in INTO THE LYON'S DEN. He broke their engagement to follow the Princess of Wales to the continent.

Bancroft, Ellis Lockhart – She's the heroine of LADY LUCK AND THE LYON, and is the Daughter of Winston Lockhart.

Bancroft, Garrick – He's the hero of LADY LUCK AND THE LYON, and is known as Viscount Lynley.

Bancroft, Stanford – He is the Duke of Asherford, and is a friend to Kingston Barclay. He appears in LOVED BY THE LYON.

Barclay, Dorena – She is the younger sister of Kingston Barclay, and appears in LOVED BY THE LYON.

Barclay, Gareth – He is the younger brother of Kingston Barclay, and appears in LOVED BY THE LYON.

Barclay, Kingston – He is the hero of LOVED BY THE LYON, and is the current Duke of Caerleon.

Barclay, Madeline – She is the younger sister of Kingston Barclay, and appears in LOVED BY THE LYON.

Barclay, Paxton – He is the younger brother of Kingston Barclay, and appears in LOVED BY THE LYON.

Barclay, Rebecca – She is the younger sister of Kingston Barclay, and appears in LOVED BY THE LYON.

Barclay, Vanessa Becket – She is the heroine of LOVED BY THE LYON, and is the Duchess of Caerleon. Her late older brother, Gabriel, was childhood best friends with Kingston Barclay.

Barker, _______________ – Lord Barker is married to Elaine Versey Barker, and appears in THE TALONS OF A LYON.

Barker, Elaine Versey – She is the younger sister of Lance and Percy Versey, and is Lady Barker. She appears in THE TALONS OF A LYON.

Barney, _________ – Mr. Barney is a kidnaper and thug, who was hired by Everett. He appears in THE LYON'S DEN IN WINTER.

Barrow, Homer – He is a Bow Street Runner, and works for the Duke of Lotheil at times. He appears in KISS OF THE LYON.

Barrymore, Amelia Fielding – She's the heroine of THE LYON'S SECRET, and is the younger sister of Josiah Barrymore's deceased best friend.

Barrymore, Josiah – He is the hero of THE LYON'S SECRET, and is currently a vicar. He also works for the Home Office as a spy.

Bassage, Adriana Stapleton Roberts – She's the heroine of THE LYON'S PUZZLE, and is the widow of a merchant, Mr. Roberts. She is also the daughter of Baron Kentwood.

Bassage, Montague – He's the hero of THE LYON'S PUZZLE, and is the 12th Earl Pennington. He is also known as the "worst man in London."

Bellamy, Belinda – She is the younger sister of Araminta Lamb, and suffers from melancholia. She appears in THE LYON AND THE LAMB.

Benton, Paul – Baron Benton was the first husband of Adriana Benton. He was a captain in the British army, and was a war hero. He was injured in the war and was an invalid towards the end of his life. He appears in THE LYON'S SHARE.

Black, Malcolm – He is the father of Viola Black Neilson, and is a solicitor by day and a consulting card sharp by night. He is the former lover of Bessie Dove-Lyon, and they are still friends. He's also known as the Silver Tongue. He appears in THE LYON'S DEN IN WINTER.

Blackwell, Florence – She is the widow of Major Blackwell, and hired Lady Emma Spencer as her paid companion after her father, Lord Seton, abandoned her. She is also the older sister of Bessie Dove-Lyon. She appears in THE LYON'S LADY LOVE.

Bouchard, Josephine – She is a friend of Moriah Henshaw, and is a member of the Wicked Widow's Club. She appears in TO CLAIM A LYON'S HEART.

Bradshaw, __________ – Lord Bradshaw, also known as "Brady", is the oldest friend of Peter Dermott, and appears in HOW TO STEAL A LYON'S FORTUNE.

Braeton, Honoria Quinn – She's the heroine of PRIDE OF LYONS, and is the daughter of a vicar. She was previously the paid companion/caretaker of Mrs. Edwards.

Braeton, Thomas – He is the hero of PRIDE OF LYONS, and is a wealthy nobleman.

Bramwell, Arden – He is the uncle of Jenny Bramwell, and appears in THE LYON'S SURPRISE.

Broadbank, Sr., Adam – He's Earl Templeton, and is the father of Colin and Edmund Broadbank. He appears in RESCUED BY THE LYON and CAPTIVATED BY THE LYON.

Broadbank, III, Adam – He's the young son of Lily Lovecote from her affair with the late Adam Broadbank, Jr. He is being raised by his aunt, Addy Fernside Broadbank. He appears in CAPTIVATED BY THE LYON.

Broadbank, Adelaide "Addy" Fernside – She's the heroine of CAPTIVATED BY THE LYON. She has been raising her nephew, son of her sister Lily Lovecote and the late Adam Broadbank, Jr.

Broadbank, Colin – He's the hero of RESCUED BY THE LYON, and is the new Viscount Moreland. He also appears in CAPTIVATED BY THE LYON.

Broadbank, Edmund, Sr. – He's the hero of CAPTIVATED BY THE LYON, and is also the younger brother of Colin Broadbank, Viscount Moreland. He also appears in RESCUED BY THE LYON.

Broadbank, Jr., Edmund – He's the firstborn son and heir of Edmund Broadbank, Sr., and his wife, Addy Broadbank. He appears in CAPTIVATED BY THE LYON.

Broadbank, Gemma Atherton – She's the heroine of RESCUED BY THE LYON, and is the daughter of wealthy Cit Mr. Atherton. She also appears in CAPTIVATED BY THE LYON.

Burwell, Francis "Frank" – He is a captain of the 8th Dragoons, and is a friend to Miles, the Duke of Goldthorpe. He appears in LYON EYES.

Campbell, Eric – He is a rich Scotsman, and is a potential suitor for Lady Diana Wade. He appears in FED TO THE LYON.

Cameron, __________ – He is the Duke of Lotheil, and is the chairman of the Royal Society. He appears in KISS OF THE LYON.

Chamberlain, Pierce – He is the Earl of Wainthorpe, and is a friend to Kingston Barclay. He appears in LOVED BY THE LYON.

Chetwynd, Araminta Lamb – She's the heroine of THE LYON AND THE LAMB, and is the widow of the late Horatio Lamb.

Chetwynd, Leo – He's the hero of THE LYON AND THE LAMB, and is the Earl of Aylsham, and Principal Trustee of Lady Aylsham's Foundling Hospital.

Chetwynd, Roland – The Honorable Roland Chetwynd is the younger, charming ne'er do well brother of Leo Chetwynd. He appears in THE LYON AND THE LAMB.

Colquehoun, Abel – He is the Marquess of Greenock, and was Lord MacGlory's favored suitor for his daughter's hand in marriage. He appears in LYON IN THE ROUGH.

Coventry, Gordon – Captain Coventry is a former naval hero, and a wounded veteran of the war. He is missing an eye, and has a useless arm. He is the London man-of-affairs for the Duke of Wyndmere. He appears in RESCUED BY THE LYON and CAPTIVATED BY THE LYON.

Crabtree, ________ – Mr. Crabtree is the father of Beverly Crabtree Glazebrook, and had eloped to marry Baron Daintith's daughter, which caused the estrangement. He appears in THE SCANDALOUS LYON.

Crabtree, ________ – Mrs. Crabtree is the estranged daughter of Baron Daintith, and is the mother of Beverly Crabtree Glazebrook. She appears in THE SCANDALOUS LYON.

Crinoline, Victoria – She's the mistress of Viscount Langdon, and is an attempted murderer. She appears in THE HEART OF A LYON.

Crossley, Ambrose – He is the 5th Earl of Pendlewood, and is known as "Pen." He is the best friend of Edward Fortescue, and appears in THE DEVILISH LYON.

Crowden, Barbara – She's the niece of Adriana Benton, and is the daughter of Lord and Lady Norbridge. She appears in THE LYON'S SHARE.

Crowden, Henry – He is Lord Norbridge, and is the father of Barbara Crowden, and the Brother-in-law of Adriana Benton. He appears in THE LYON'S SHARE.

Crowden, Liza – She is Lady Norbridge, and is the sister of Adriana Benton, and the mother of Barbara Crowden. She appears in THE LYON'S SHARE.

Culkins, ________ – Major Culkins is a family friend to Colonel and Mrs. Sinclair, and appears in THE COURAGE OF A LYON.

Cunningham, Marjorie – Lady Cunningham appears in LYON IN THE ROUGH, and was hoping to marry Lucas Lyon.

Daintith, _________ – Baron Daintith is the father of Mrs. Crabtree (his estranged daughter), and is the grandfather of Beverly Crabtree Glazebrook. He appears in THE SCANDALOUS LYON.

Danford, Caroline – Lady Danford is the daughter of Mrs. Edwards, and appears in PRIDE OF LYONS.

Danford, Louis – Lord Danford was the employer of Honoria Quinn, and appears in PRIDE OF LYONS.

Darby, ________ – Mr. Darby is the elderly father of Rebecca Darby. He appears in ALWAYS THE LYON TAMER.

Dawkins, William – He is a friend to Mason Redstone, and is the Marquess of Easton. He appears in A LYON'S PRIDE.

Dawson, Phoebe – She is the Countess of Southwood, and is the mother of Olivia Dawson. She appears in THE HEART OF A LYON.

Dawson, Simon – He's the Earl of Southwood, and is the father of Olivia Dawson. He appears in THE HEART OF A LYON.

De Coucy, Louis – He is the uncle of Audrey Ruston, and is an art dealer and collector in HOW TO STEAL A LYON'S FORTUNE.

de Villiers, Francesca – She is the mother of Lily de Villiers Diamond Redstone. She later becomes a famous courtesan at the Lyon's Den, known as "La Flamme." She appears in A LYON'S PRIDE and LYON OF THE HIGHLANDS.

Dermott, Audrey Ruston – Heroine of HOW TO STEAL A LYON'S FORTUNE. She is the former stepdaughter of Vincent Lyon, who is the nephew of the late Sandstrom Lyon; husband of Bessie Dove-Lyon.

Dermott, Leona – She is the younger sister of Peter Dermott, and appears in HOW TO STEAL A LYON'S FORTUNE.

Dermott, Peter – Hero of HOW TO STEAL A LYON'S FORTUNE, he is an honorable baron, and is a guardian to his younger sister and niece.

Devereaux, Barbara Versey – She is the eldest daughter of Percy and Aurelia Versey, the Duke and Duchess of Dellborough, and is married to Lord Devereaux. She appears in THE TALONS OF THE LYON.

Dewar, Simon – He is Viscount Lowry, and appears in LYON OF THE HIGHLANDS. He was hoping to be a suitor for Mina Redstone's hand in marriage.

Dorchester, Philip – He is a cousin to Garrick Bancroft, and appears in LADY LUCK AND THE LYON.

Dove-Lyon, Bessie – She is the mysterious widow of Colonel Sandstrom T. Lyon, who was rumored to be a much older man. She is also known as the Black Widow of Whitehall, and is the owner of the Lyon's Den. In THE LYON'S LADY LOVE it is revealed she has an older and estranged sister named Florence

Blackwell. Their parents were criminals. Bessie had killed her father and ran away from the crime scene. In HOW TO STEAL A LYON'S FORTUNE, her late husband's nephew, Vincent Lyon, is in possession of a nude painting of her when she was a courtesan. She also removes her veil when speaking of family matters with Audrey Ruston (former stepdaughter of her nephew, Vincent Lyon). She is present in every novel in this series and is usually heavily veiled in black from head to toe. In PRETTY LITTLE LYON it is revealed that she is the birth mother of Charlotta "Lottie" Walcot. She sets up her daughter with her childhood love interest, Septimus Grey, who is also an investigator for Mrs. Dove-Lyon. Charlotta's father had an affair with Mrs. Dove Lyon when she was a courtesan. In THE LYON'S SECRET, her childhood friend, Mrs. Fielding, is the mother of Amelia Fielding.

Drake, Evan – He is the Marquess of Merrick, and is married to Rachel Drake. He appears in THE LYON'S LADY LOVE.

Drake, Rachel – She is the Marchioness of Merrick, and is married to Evan Drake. She appears in THE LYON'S LADY LOVE.

Drayton, Henry – He is the Duke of Westbury, and is a friend of neighbor of Mason Redstone. He appears in A LYON'S PRIDE.

Drayton, Jeanette – She is the Duchess of Westbury, and is a friend of neighbor of Mason Redstone. She appears in A LYON'S PRIDE.

Drinkwater, _______________ – Mrs. Drinkwater is the cook and housekeeper at the vicarage, and also helps Josiah Barrymore with his clandestine jobs. She appears in THE LYON'S SECRET.

Easton, Madeline Keyes – She's the heroine of TAMED BY THE LYON, and is the daughter of William Keyes. She also appears in LADY LUCK AND THE LYON.

Easton, Oliver – He's the hero of TAMED BY THE LYON, and is the Earl of Foxmore.

Edwards, ________ – Mrs. Edwards is the mother of Lady Danford, and appears in PRIDE OF LYONS.

Edwards, Rose – She is the best friend of Evangeline Prescott, and appears in THE LYON'S LAIRD.

Elligon, Owen – He is the older stepbrother of Vanessa Becket, and appears in LOVED BY THE LYON.

Evans, Winston – He is an MP for the Berkshire district, and is a friend and neighbor of Peter Ravenshaw. He appears in THE LYON SLEEPS TONIGHT.

Farthingale, Lily – She is a bright intellectual who attended the Royal Society lecture given by Professor Lyon. She appears in KISS OF THE LYON.

Fielding, James – He is the older reprobate brother of Amelia Fielding Barrymore, and appears in THE LYON'S SECRET.

Finster, ________ – Lord Finster was a possible suitor for Jenny Bramwell, and appears in THE LYON'S SURPRISE.

Ford, John – He is a Bow Street Runner, hired to solve the attempted murder of the Duke of Kendall. He appears in THE HEART OF A LYON.

Fortescue, Charles Francis – He is the oldest twin and heir to his parents, Edward and Harriet Hurst Fortescue. He appears in THE DEVILISH LYON.

Fortescue, Edward – He is the hero of THE DEVILISH LYON, and is Viscount Eskdale. He was a widower, and is known as the Fallen Angel of Mayfair.

Fortescue, Harriet Hurst – She is the heroine of THE DEVLISH LYON. She was the younger sister of the late Baron Huxley, friend of Edward Fortescue.

Fortescue, Sophia Elizabeth – She is the younger twin of her parents, Edward and Harriet Hurst Fortescue. She appears in THE DEVIL-ISH LYON.

Foxx, Michael – He is a Bow Street Runner, hired to solve the attempted murder of the Duke of Kendall. He appears in THE HEART OF A LYON

Fraser, _____________ – He is the Duke of Molineux, and is a friend to Duncan MacLeish. He appears in LYON OF THE HIGHLANDS.

Frogmore, Hannah – She is the eldest daughter of the late Henry Frogmore, and his wife, Seraphina Frogmore Versey. She appears in THE TALONS OF THE LYON.

Frogmore, Harry – He is the young son and heir of the late Henry Frogmore, and his wife, Seraphina Frogmore Versey. He is the current Baron Frogmore, and appears in THE TALONS OF THE LYON.

Frogmore, Helena – She is the younger daughter of the late Henry Frogmore, and his wife, Seraphina Frogmore Versey. She appears in THE TALONS OF THE LYON.

Frogmore, Marcus – He is the brother-in-law to Seraphina Frogmore, and appears in THE TALONS OF THE LYON.

Frogmore, Virginia – She is the wife of Marcus Frogmore, and appears in THE TALONS OF THE LYON.

George, MaryAnne – She is the chaperone to Beverly Crabtree, and was interested in Mr. Anthony Perlew. She appears in THE SCANDALOUS LYON.

Glazebrook, Beverly Crabtree – She is the heroine of THE SCANDALOUS LYON, and is the granddaughter of Baron Daintith.

Glazebrook, Charles – He is the older brother of Jason Glazebrook, and appears in THE SCANDALOUS LYON.

Glazebrook, Jason – Hero of THE SCANDALOUS LYON. He is the younger brother of Charles Glazebrook, the Duke of Shrewsbury.

Gold, _____________ – Mr. Gold is Amber Gohar's father. He appears in INTO THE LYON'S DEN.

Gold, ____________ – Mr. Gold is Amber Gohar's grandfather. He appears in INTO THE LYON'S DEN.

Goldthorpe, _______ – She is the dowager Duchess of Goldthorpe, and is the mother of Miles and Cecilia. She appears in LYON EYES.

Goldthorpe, Cecilia – She is the sister of Miles, Duke of Goldthorpe, and appears in LYON EYES.

Goldthorpe, Jenny Hambling – She is the heroine of LYON EYES, and is the wealthy heiress Of her father's mills.

Goldthorpe, Miles – He is the hero of LYON EYES, and is the Duke of Goldthorpe.

Gordon, ____________ – Lord Gordon is the father of Nessie, and grandfather of the current Earl of Walden, Lord Stefan. He is trying to become his legal guardian to control his fortune. He appears in LYON HEARTED.

Grey, Charlotta "Lottie" Walcot – She's the heroine of PRETTY LITTLE LYON, and is the birth daughter of Mrs. Bessie Dove-Lyon.

Grey, Septimus – He is the hero of PRETTY LITTLE LYON, and is known as Baron Grey. He Was the former student of Bertram Walcot. He marries the daughter of Mrs. Bessie Dove-Lyon.

Grisham, _________ – Lady Romney is the mother of Charlotte Grisham Prescott, and Lord Jason Grisham, presumptive heir of his missing brother, Matthew Grisham. She appears in LYON'S PREY.

Grisham, Jason – He is the youngest child of Lady Romney, and is the presumptive heir of his brother, Matthew Grisham. He appears in LYON'S PREY.

Hamilton, Avery – He is a former lover of Evangeline Prescott, and appears in THE LYON'S LAIRD.

Hamilton, Grace – She is a friend to Amelia Fielding Barrymore in the parish of Upper Wexham. She appears in THE LYON'S SECRET.

Hanson, ___________ – Mr. Hanson is a traitor, and appears in THE LYON'S SECRET.

Harkwell, ___________ – He is an unsuitable suitor for the hand of Gemma Atherton. He is approved of by Mr. Atherton, but not by Gemma. He appears in RESCUED BY THE LYON.

Harrington, ___________ – He is a disreputable gambler at the Lyon's Den. He appears in FED TO THE LYON.

Hart, Dexter – He is a banker, and is a friend to Mason Redstone. He appears in A LYON'S PRIDE.

Haverfield, ___________ – He is the Earl of Haverfield, and is the father of Simon Haverfield and Danielle Haverfield Lyon. He appears in KISS OF THE LYON.

Haverfield, Josiah – He is the younger brother of the Earl of Haverfield, and is uncle to Simon Haverfield and Danielle Haverfield Lyon. He appears in KISS OF THE LYON.

Haverfield, Simon – He is Viscount Royston, and is the older brother of Danielle Haverfield Lyon. He appears in KISS OF THE LYON.

Haverford, ___________ – He is the Duke of Haverford, and is a friend to the Versey family. He appears in THE TALONS OF THE LYON.

Haverford, ___________ – She is the Duchess of Haverford, and is a friend to the Versey family. She appears in THE TALONS OF THE LYON.

Hawley, Gyles – He is a friend of Vincent St. John, and is the Marquis of Wickes. He appears in TO CLAIM A LYON'S HEART.

Hawthorne, ___________ – Mrs. Hawthorne is the mother of Emiline Hawthorne Quinton, and appears in A LYON IN HER BED.

Herndon, Miles – He is Lord Armstrong, and is a friend to Leo Thurston-Hunter. He appears in FALL OF THE LYON.

Honeyfield, Amber – She was formerly engaged to Miles Rutherford. She appears in THE LYON SLEEPS TONIGHT.

Honeywell, __________ – Lord Honeywell is a disreputable suitor for Lily Lovecote's hand. He appears in CAPTIVATED BY THE LYON.

Hough, Diana Rees – She is Lady Dunnamore, and is the sister of Elliott Rees. She married an elderly man three times her age. She appears in INTO THE LYON'S DEN.

Hough, Geoffrey – He is the son and heir of Lord Dunnamore. His stepmother is Lady Diana Dunnamore, sister to Elliott Rees. He appears in INTO THE LYON'S DEN.

Huntington, Catherine "Kit" – She is a client of Mrs. Bessie Dove-Lyon, and is a new friend to Addy Fernside Broadbank. She appears in CAPTIVATED BY THE LYON.

John, ____________ – Dowager Countess of Morthan. She is an elderly lady with a cane. She appears in INTO THE LYON'S DEN.

John, ____________ – Lord Morthan. He is the son of the dowager Countess of Morthan. He appears in INTO THE LYON'S DEN.

Jones, Beatrice – She is the mother of Opal Jones, and appears in THE LYON SLEEPS TONIGHT.

Jones, Sinclair – He was a former major in the army, and is the father of Opal Jones. He appears in THE LYON SLEEPS TONIGHT.

Jupp, Christopher – He is the son and heir of Lord Portham, and was an romantic interest for Amber Gohar in INTO THE LYON'S DEN.

Kelly, Wilfred – He is the son of a local squire, and has part interest in the mills of Mr. Hambling. He is trying to coerce Jenny Hambling into marrying him, and appears in LYON EYES.

Kent, __________ – Lord Kent fought a duel with and fatally wounded the Duke of Surrey. He appears in TO TAME THE LYON.

Kenwreck, ___________ – Lady Kenwreck is the sponsor of the Home for Desolate Ladies. She appears in HOW TO STEAL A LYON'S FORTUNE.

Kenwreck, ___________ – Lord Kenwreck is the husband of Lady Kenwreck, and appears in HOW TO STEAL A LYON'S FORTUNE.

Kettering, Oliver – He is Viscount Roxbury, and is one of the "Brothers Bachelor." He appears in THE LYON SLEEPS TO-NIGHT.

Keyes, Alice – She is the second wife of William Keyes, and is the stepmother of Madeline Keyes Easton and Coraline Keyes Wortham. She appears in TAMED BY THE LYON.

Keyes, William – He is the father of Madeline Keyes Easton, and Coraline Keyes Wortham. He appears in TAMED BY THE LYON.

King, Gavin – He is a Bow Street Runner, and appears in RESCUED BY THE LYON and CAPTIVATED BY THE LYON.

Lacey, Grace – She is a friend to Moriah Henshaw, and is married to Lord Nicholas Lacey. She appears in TO CLAIM A LYON'S HEART.

Lacey, Nicholas – He is a friend of Moriah Henshaw, and is married to Grace Lacey. He appears in TO CLAIM A LYON'S HEART.

Langdale, _________ – Baron Langdale is the brother of Lady Romney, and is the temporary guardian for Jason Grisham, the heir presumptive to Lord Romneys title. He appears in LYON'S PREY.

Langdon, Dillon – Viscount Langdon is a card cheat, and was trying to force Lord Southwood to offer his daughter, Olivia Dawson, to be his wife. He appears in THE HEART OF A LYON.

Lennox, Charlotte – She is the Duchess of Mercia, and is the wife of William Lennox. She appears in ALWAYS THE LYON TAMER.

Lennox, John – He is the hero of ALWAYS THE LYON TAMER, and is the brother of the Duke of Mercia. He is also known as the "Lion of the Lennoxes."

Lennox, Prudence – She is the younger sister of William Lennox and John Lennox. She appears in ALWAYS THE LYON TAMER.

Lennox, Rebecca Darby – She is the heroine of ALWAYYS THE LYON TAMER.

Lennox, William – He is the Duke of Mercia, and is the brother of John Lennox. He appears In ALWAYS THE LYON TAMER.

Lerwich, ________ – He is a reprobate and is a friend of Prinny. He appears in LYON HEARTED.

Lewis, Hiram – He is a Bow Street Runner, and appears in INTO THE LYON OF FIRE.

Leyland, ________ – Mr. Leyland is a wealthy American art collector, and appears in HOW TO STEAL A LYON'S FORTUNE.

Lockhart, Leighton – She's a younger sister of Ellis Lockhart Bancroft, and appears in LADY LUCK AND THE LYON.

Lockhart, Marianne – She's the mother of Ellis, Leighton, Parker, and Merritt Lockhart. She was also hidden from her daughters in an asylum by her estranged husband, Winston Lockhart. She appears in LADY LUCK AND THE LYON.

Lockhart, Merritt – She's a younger sister of Ellis Lockhart Bancroft, and appears in LADY LUCK AND THE LYON.

Lockhart, Parker – She's a younger sister of Ellis Lockhart Bancroft, and appears in LADY LUCK AND THE LYON.

Lockhart, Winston – He's the father of Ellis, Leighton, Parker, and Merritt Lockhart. He appears in LADY LUCK AND THE LYON.

Longford, Geoffrey – He's the best friend of Lord Braeton, and appears in PRIDE OF LYONS.

Lovecote, Lily – She is the younger sister of Addy Fernside Broadbank, and is an actress. She is also the mother of Adam Broadbank, III, through her affair with the late Adam Broadbank, Jr. She appears in CAPTIVATED BY THE LYON.

Lyon, Beatrix MacGlory – She's the heroine of LYON IN THE ROUGH, and is the only child of Lord MacGlory.

Lyon, Cheyne – He is the hero of THE LYON'S SURPRISE, and is the Duke of Mar. He is the older brother of Matthew, Lucas, and John Lyon. He also appears in LYON IN THE ROUGH.

Lyon, Danielle Haverfield – She is the heroine of KISS OF THE LYON. She is the daughter of the Earl of Haverfield, and is the younger sister of Viscount Royston, Simon Haverfield. She also appears in LYON IN THE ROUGH.

Lyon, Fionn – He is the eldest child and heir of Cheyne and Jenny Lyon, and appears in LYON IN THE ROUGH.

Lyon, Jenny Bradford – She's the wife of John Lyon, and is the mother of Johnny Lyon. She appears in THE LYON'S SURPRISE.

Lyon, Jenny Bramwell – She's the heroine of THE LYON'S SURPRISE, and is the daughter of an Oxford professor. She is also the best friend of Jenny Bradford Lyon. She also appears in LYON IN THE ROUGH.

Lyon, John – He is the younger brother of Cheyne Lyon, and is married to Jenny Bradford Lyon, and are the parents of Johnny Lyon. He appears in THE LYON'S SURPRISE.

Lyon, Johnny – He is the son of John Lyon and Jenny Bradford Lyon. He appears in THE LYON'S SURPRISE.

Lyon, Lucas – He is the hero of LYON IN THE ROUGH, and is the younger brother of Cheyne and Matthew Lyon. He also appears in THE LYON'S SURPRISE.

Lyon, Matthew – Hero of KISS OF THE LYON. His granduncle is the late Sandstrom Lyon, so he is related to Bessie Dove-Lyon. His brother is the Duke of Mar. He is a mathematics professor at the

University of Edinburgh. He also appears in THE LYON'S SUR-PRISE and LYON IN THE ROUGH.

Lyon, Vincent – He is the unscrupulous former stepfather of Audrey Ruston, and is the nephew of the late Sandstrom Lyon; husband to Bessie Dove-Lyon.

MacGlory, __________ – Lord MacGlory is the father of Beatrix MacGlory and is the husband of Lottie MacGlory. He is the head of the Royal Bank of Scotland, and appears in LYON IN THE ROUGH.

MacGlory, Lottie – She is the stepmother of Beatrix MacGlory, and is a cousin of the late Jocelyn MacGlory and to Harriet Rochester. She appears in LYON IN THE ROUGH.

MacLauchlin, Andrew – He was the late older brother of Isaac MacLauchlin. He appears in TO TAME THE LYON.

MacLauchlin, Blake – He is the Scottish cousin of Andrew and Isaac MacLauchlin, and is known as Viscount Lorne. He prefers to go by Lord MacLauchlin. He appears in TO TAME THE LYON. He later marries the former Duchess of Surrey's maid, Maude.

MacLauchlin, Clara Ainsworth – She is the heroine of TO TAME THE LYON. She was formerly the Duchess of Surrey. She was the childhood friend of Isaac MacLauchlin.

MacLauchlin, Isaac – He's the hero of TO TAME THE LYON, and is the Marquess of Durham. He was childhood friends with the Clara, the former Duchess of Surrey.

MacLauchlin, Maude – She was the former wet nurse and teacher to Mabel Ainsworth, daughter of the late Duke of Surrey, and his wife, the Duchess of Surrey. She later became the Duchess' lady's maid and friend. She marries Black MacLauchlin, who is Lord MacLauchlin, and resides in their Scottish castle. She appears in TO TAME THE LYON.

Maclean, Adele – She is the sister of Laird Maclean, and appears in THE LYON'S LAIRD.

Maclean, Camren – Hero of THE LYON'S LAIRD. He is the head of Clan Maclean in Scotland.

Maclean, Cowan – He is the youngest brother of Camren Maclean, and is known to be a pirate. He appears in THE LYON'S LAIRD.

Maclean, Evangeline – Heroine of THE LYON'S LAIRD. She is the spinster daughter of wealthy parents.

Maclean, Ian – He is the brother of Laird Camren, and appears in THE LYON'S LAIRD.

Maclean, Mariel – She is Laird Camren's mother, and appears in THE LYON'S LAIRD.

Maclean, Sencha – She is the wife of Ian Maclean, sister-in-law of Camren Maclean, and appears in THE LYON'S LAIRD.

MacLeish, Callum – He is the younger brother of Duncan MacLeish, and appears in LYON OF THE HIGHLANDS. He is married to Flora MacLeish.

MacLeish, Duncan – He's the hero of LYON OF THE HIGHLANDS, and is the Laird of Kilduggan Castle.

MacLeish, Flora – She is the wife of Callum MacLeish, and appears in LYON OF THE HIGHLANDS.

MacLeish, Hamish – He is the firstborn son and heir of Laird Duncan MacLeish, and his wife, Mina Redstone MacLeish. He appears in LYON OF THE HIGHLANDS.

MacLeish, Jamie – He is the firstborn son and heir of Callum and Flora MacLeish, and appears in LYON OF THE HIGHLANDS.

MacLeish, Shona – She is the young daughter of Callum and Flora MacLeish, and appears in LYON OF THE HIGHLANDS.

MacLeish, Wilhelmina "Mina" Redstone – She's the heroine of LYON OF THE HIGHLANDS, and was previously the widow of the Earl of Redstone. She also appeared in A LYON'S PRIDE.

MacRaine, Sally – She is a wealthy woolen heiress, and is a friend to Beatrix MacGlory in LYON IN THE ROUGH.

Manning, __________ – Lord Manning is the person in charge at the Home Office. He appears in KISS OF THE LYON.

Masterson, Gray – Sir Gray is head of the division at the Home Office that Josiah Barrymore reports to. He appears in THE LYON'S SECRET.

Monroe, Lady Fern – She is the sister of Olivia Prescott, and is the mother of Miss Prudence. She appears in THE LYON'S LAIRD.

Monroe, Lord – He is the husband of Lady Monroe, and is the father of Miss Prudence. He appears in THE LYON'S LAIRD.

Monroe, Prudence – She is the daughter of Lord and Lady Monroe, and is the first cousin of Evangeline Prescott. She appears in THE LYON'S LAIRD.

Moore, Patricia – She is a friend of Moriah Henshaw, and is a member of the Wicked Widow's Club. She appears in TO CLAIM A LYON'S HEART.

Neilson, Constance – She is the only child of Duncan Neilson and his late wife, Amelia. She appears in THE LYON'S DEN IN WINTER.

Neilson, Duncan – He is the hero of THE LYON'S DEN IN WINTER, and is a widowed physician based in Scotland.

Neilson, Viola Black – She is the heroine of THE LYON'S DEN IN WINTER, and is a writer of plays.

O'Riley, Mark – He was a corporal in the British army, and the valet to the late Colonel Sinclair. He later becomes the valet to Captain Charles Audley. He appears in THE COURAGE OF A LYON.

Page, Adam – He is the son of Matthew Page, who was the former best friend of Roger, the Earl of Harrowby (the estranged grandfather of Moriah Henshaw). He was also the former lover of Moriah Henshaw. He appears in TO CLAIM A LYON'S HEART.

Patterson, Regina – She's the former mistress of Vincent St. John, and appears in TO CLAIM A LYON'S HEART.

Perlew, Anthony – He is a possible suitor for Beverly Crabtree, but was interested in her chaperone, MaryAnne George. He appears in THE SCANDALOUS LYON.

Powell, Emma Spencer – She is the heroine of THE LYON'S LADY LOVE, and is the Countess of Rutherford. She is the daughter of Lord Seton.

Powell, Marcus – He is the hero of THE LYON'S LADY LOVE, and is the Earl of Rutherford.

Prescott, ________ – She's the Dowager Countess of Clarendon, and is the mother of Evan Prescott and Lady Catherine Rivers. She appears in LYON'S PREY.

Prescott, Amelia – She's the first wife of Evan Prescott, Lord Clarendon, and died giving birth to their son and heir, Edward Prescott. She appeared in LYON'S PREY.

Prescott, Charlotte – She's the heroine of LYON'S PREY, and is the second wife of Evan Prescott. She's also the daughter of Lord and Lady Romney.

Prescott, Edward – He's the first son and heir of Evan and Amelia Prescott. He appears in LYON'S PREY.

Prescott, Evan – He's the hero of LYON'S PREY, and is the 5th Earl of Clarendon.

Prescott, Forest – He is the father of Evangeline Prescott, and appears in THE LYON'S LAIRD.

Prescott, Olivia – She is the mother of Evangeline Prescott, and is the sister of Lady Monroe. She appears in THE LYON'S LAIRD.

Quinn, Aeneas – He is the father of Honoria Quinn. He is also a vicar, and appears in PRIDE OF LYONS.

Quinn, Anne – She is the mother of Honoria Quinn, and appears in PRIDE OF LYONS.

Quinton, Emiline Hawthorne – She is the heroine of A LYON IN HER BED, and is the daughter of a physician.

Quinton, George – He is the second child and heir of Leo and Emiline Quinton. He appears In A LYON IN HER BED.

Quinton, Leonard "Leo" – He is the hero of A LYON IN HER BED, and is the 6th Earl of Morton.

Quinton, Mary – She is the eldest child and daughter of Leo and Emiline Quinton. She appears in A LYON IN HER BED.

Ramsden, Beaumont "Beau" – He is the Marquess of Hexhaven, and is a client of Ms. Bessie Dove-Lyon. He appears in LADY LUCK AND THE LYON.

Ravenshaw, ____________ – Mrs. Ravenshaw is the mother of Peter Ravenshaw. She is widowed and is living at their estate in the Berkshires. She appears in THE LYON SLEEPS TONIGHT.

Ravenshaw, Opal Jones – Heroine of THE LYON SLEEPS TO-NIGHT, and daughter of a former major in the army. She was a childhood friend of Peter Ravenshaw.

Ravenshaw, Peter – Hero of THE LYON SLEEPS TONIGHT, and former captain in the army. He was a childhood friend of Opal Jones.

Redstone, Amelia – She is the twin daughter of Mason Redstone and Lily de Villiers Diamond Redstone. She appears in A LYON'S PRIDE and in LYON OF THE HIGHLANDS.

Redstone, Belinda – She is the twin daughter of Mason Redstone and Lily de Villiers Diamond Redstone. She appears in A LYON'S PRIDE and LYON OF THE HIGHLANDS.

Redstone, Francesco – He's the third child and firstborn son of Mason and Lily Redstone, the current Earl and Countess of Redstone. He appears in LYON OF THE HIGHLANDS.

Redstone, Lily de Villiers Diamond – Heroine of A LYON'S PRIDE, she was the childhood sweetheart of Mason Redstone. She's also the mother of twin daughters from Mason Redstone. She also appeared in LYON OF THE HIGHLANDS.

Redstone, Mason – Hero of A LYON'S PRIDE, and the Earl of Redstone. He was the childhood sweetheart of Lily de Villiers (Diamond), and is the father of her twin daughters. He also appears in LYON OF THE HIGHLANDS.

Redstone, Wilhelmina "Mina" – She is the stepmother of Mason Redstone, and is the dowager Countess of Redstone. She appears in A LYON'S PRIDE.

Rees, ____________ – Dowager Countess of Byrn. She is the mother of Elliott Rees, Lady Diana Dunnamore, and Gwen Rees. She appears in INTO THE LYON'S DEN.

Rees, Amber Gohar – Heroine of INTO THE LYON'S DEN, and now the Countess of Byrn. She married Elliott Rees, Lord Byrn. She was a jeweler in her family's business, the Dragon Hoard.

Rees, Elliott – Hero of INTO THE LYON'S DEN, and the Earl of Byrn. He married Amber Gohar, the jeweler in her family's business, The Dragon Hoard, in the Lyon's Den.

Rivers, Catherine – Lady Rivers is the sister of Evan Prescott, and appears in LYON'S PREY.

Rivers, Tom – Lord Rivers is the husband of Catherine Rivers, and is the brother-in-law of Evan Prescott. He appears in LYON'S PREY.

Rochdale, _________ – Lord Rochdale is the brother-in-law of Lord Braeton, and appears in PRIDE OF LYONS.

Rochdale, Joanna – Lady Rochdale is the sister of Lord Braeton, and appears in PRIDE OF LYONS.

Rochester, Harriet – Lady Rochester is the sister of the late Jocelyn MacGlory, and is the aunt to Beatrix MacGlory. She appears in LYON IN THE ROUGH.

Rolston, Crispin – He is the Duke of Bainbridge, and is a friend to Kingston Barclay. He appears in LOVED BY THE LYON.

Rutherford, Miles – He is the Earl of Harcourt, and is one of the "Brothers Bachelor." He was formerly engaged to Lady Amber Honeyfield, and appears in THE LYON SLEEPS TONIGHT.

Rydell, James – He is a younger son of Phyllida Rydell, and appears in INTO THE LYON OF FIRE.

Rydell, Mark – He is the second son of the late Duke and Duchess of Embleton, and is younger than his brother, Matthew Rydell, the current Duke of Embleton. He appears in INTO THE LYON OF FIRE.

Rydell, Matthew – He's the hero of INTO THE LYON OF FIRE, and is the newly invested Duke of Embleton after the passing of his father, the previous duke.

Rydell, Paul – He is a younger son of Phyllida Rydell, and appears in INTO THE LYON OF FIRE.

Rydell, Peter – He is a younger son of Phyllida Rydell, and appears in INTO THE LYON OF FIRE.

Rydell, Phyllida – She's the dowager Duchess of Embleton, and is the mother of Matthew Rydell and his other siblings. She appears in INTO THE LYON OF FIRE.

Rydell, Robert – He is the firstborn son and heir of the current Duke and Duchess of Embleton, Matthew and Sarah Rydell. He appears in INTO THE LYON OF FIRE.

Rydell, Sarah Ainsworth – She's the heroine of INTO THE LYON OF FIRE. She was also the widow of the late Earl of Crewood.

Rydell, Theophilus – He is a younger son of Phyllida Rydell, and appears in INTO THE LYON OF FIRE.

Rydell, Timothy – He is a younger son of Phyllida Rydell, and appears in INTO THE LYON OF FIRE.

Shipley, Cedric – Lord Shipley is the husband of Joanna Shipley, who is the best friend of Harriet Hurst. He appears in THE DEVILISH LYON.

Shipley, Joanna – Lady Shipley is the best friend of Harriet Hurst, and appears in THE DEVILISH LYON.

Sinclair, Elias – Colonel Sinclair served in the British army and passed away after the Battle of Waterloo. His daughter, Amy Sinclair, was a nurse in the army. He appears in THE COURAGE OF A LYON.

Sinclair, Margaret – She is the widow of Colonel Sinclair, and is the mother of Amy Sinclair. She appears in THE COURAGE OF THE LYON.

Snead, Neville – He is the son of Roger Snead, and is the nephew of Sir William Ashby. He appears in FALL OF THE LYON.

Snead, Roger – He is the half-brother of Sir William Ashby, and is the father of Neville Snead. He appears in FALL OF THE LYON.

Somerford, Richard – He's the younger son of a viscount, and is a potential suitor for Adriana Stapleton's hand in marriage. He appears in THE LYON'S PUZZLE.

Spencer, _________ – He is Lord Seton, and is the father of Lady Emma Spencer. He appears in THE LYON'S LADY LOVE.

Spencer, _________ – She is Lady Seton, and is the stepmother of Lady Emma Spencer. She appears in THE LYON'S LADY LOVE.

St. Clair, Caroline – She is the Countess of Mayfield, and is married to Luke St. Clair. She appears in THE LYON'S LADY LOVE.

St. Clair, Catherine – She is the Duchess of Everton, and is married to Luke St. Clair. She appears in THE LYON'S LADY LOVE.

St. Clair, Jeremy – He is the Duke of Everton, and is married to Catherine St. Clair. He is also the brother of Luke St. Clair and Laurel St. Clair. He appears in THE LYON'S LADY LOVE.

St. Clair, Laurel – She is the illegitimate half-sister of Jeremy and Luke St. Clair. She appears in THE LYON'S LADY LOVE.

St. Clair, Luke – He is the Earl of Mayfield, and is married to Caroline St. Clair. He is also the brother of Jeremy St. Clair and Laurel St. Clair. He appears in THE LYON'S LADY LOVE.

St. John, Charles – He's the father of Vincent St. John, and is currently the duke. He appears in TO CLAIM A LYON'S HEART.

St. John, Moriah Henshaw – She's the heroine of TO CLAIM A LYON'S HEART, and is the best friend of Seraphina Frogmore Versey. She is the estranged niece of Aurelia Versey, Duchess of Dellborough. She also appears in THE TALONS OF A LYON.

St. John, Rachel – She's the mother of Vincent St. John, and is currently the duchess. She appears in TO CLAIM A LYON'S HEART.

St. John, Vincent – He's the hero of TO CLAIM A LYON'S HEART, and is the best friend of Lance Versey. His title is the Marquis of Saxton, and is the heir to his father's dukedom. He also appears in THE TALONS OF A LYON.

Stanley, Amanda – She is the sister of Marcus Powell, the Earl of Rutherford, and is married to Lord Stanley. She appears in THE LYON'S LADY LOVE.

Stanley, _________ – Lord Stanley is married to Lady Amanda Stanley, the sister of the Earl of Rutherford. He appears in THE LYON'S LADY LOVE.

Stanton, Albert – He's the current Duke of Kendall, after his father died when his ship was struck with a mortar shell. He appears in THE HEART OF A LYON.

Stanton, Caroline – She is the dowager Duchess of Kendall, and is the mother of Albert, Henry, Roger, and Lauren Stanton. She appears in THE HEART OF A LYON.

Stanton, Henry – He is the hero of THE HEART OF A LYON, and is the Earl of Egerton, and the younger brother of the Duke of Kendall.

Stanton, Lauren – She is the younger sister of Albert, Henry, and Roger Stanton. She appears in THE HEART OF A LYON.

Stanton, Lawrence – He was the former Duke of Kendall, and died on a ship after he picked up Henry and Roger Stanton from the battlefield. He appears in THE HEART OF THE LYON.

Stanton, Olivia Dawson – She is the heroine of THE HEART OF A LYON, and is the daughter of Lord and Lady Southwood.

Stanton, Roger – He is the younger adopted brother of Albert, Henry, and Lauren Stanton. the Duke and Duchess of Kendall adopted him when they found out he was a street child and had no parents. He appears in THE HEART OF A LYON.

Stapleton, _____________ – He's Baron Kentwood, and is the father of Adriana Stapleton and Sybil Stapleton. He appears in THE LYON'S PUZZLE.

Stapleton, _____________ – She's Baroness Kentwood, and is the mother of Adriana Stapleton and Sybil Stapleton. She appears in THE LYON'S PUZZLE.

Stapleton, Sybil – She's the younger sister of Adriana Stapleton, and appears in THE LYON'S PUZZLE.

Steere, Augusta – She is a twin daughter of Lord and Lady Steere, and appears in PRETTY LITTLE LYON.

Steere, Delphi – She is a twin daughter of Lord and Lady Steere, and appears in PRETTY LITTLE LYON.

Steere, Everard Walcot – Lord Steere is the older brother of Bertram Walcot; the husband of Lady Mary Steere, and the father of Parthenia, Delphi, and Augusta. He appears in PRETTY LITTLE LYON.

Steere, Mary – Lady Mary Steere is the sister-in-law of Bertram Walcot, and is the wife of Viscount Steere. She's the mother of Parthenia, Delphi, and Augusta. She appears in PRETTY LITTLE LYON.

Steere, Parthenia – She is the oldest daughter of Lord and Lady Steere, and is the cousin of Charlotta "Lottie" Walcot. She appears in PRETTY LITTLE LYON.

Stonehurst, Eugenie – She's the aunt of Ellis, Leighton, Parker, and Merritt Lockhart. She appears in LADY LUCK AND THE LYON.

Sutherland, Gideon – He is a friend of Camren Maclean, and is from the same clan. He appears in THE LYON'S LAIRD.

Thornton, William – He is the 5th Earl of Battersea, and is the former brother-in-law of Edward Fortescue. He appears in THE DEVIL-ISH LYON.

Thurston-Hunter, Julia – She is the younger half-sister of Leo Thurston-Hunter, and appears in FALL OF THE LYON.

Thurston-Hunter, Leander "Leo" – He is the hero of FALL OF THE LYON, and is also Viscount Amberley. He also appears in TAMED BY THE LYON.

Thurston-Hunter, Louisa – She is the younger half-sister of Leo Thurston-Hunter, and appears in FALL OF THE LYON.

Thurston-Hunter, Margaret Upshaw – She is the heroine of FALL OF THE LYON, and is now Viscountess Amberley. She was also the stepdaughter of Sir William Ashby. She also appears in TAMED BY THE LYON.

Toussaint, Emily – She is the mother of Anna Toussaint, and was the former French tutor to Frank Webb, now the current Viscount De-Wold. She appears in LYON AT THE ALTAR.

Tyler, Asher – He is a friend of Vincent St. John, and is the Earl of Rowley. He appears in TO CLAIM A LYON'S HEART.

Varley, Hugh – He is the eldest son and heir of Baron Danforth, and is a "sham" suitor for Harriet Hurst's hand in THE DEVILISH LYON.

Vaughn, _________ – Lady Vaughn is the friend of Harriet Hurst's parents. She appears in THE DEVILISH LYON.

Vaughn, ________ – Lord Vaughn is the friend of Harriet Hurst's parents. He appears in THE DEVILISH LYON.

Vaughn, Cassandra – She is a friend of Moriah Henshaw, and is the leader of the Wicked Widow's Club. She appears in TO CLAIM A LYON'S HEART.

Versey, Aurelia – She is married to Percy Versey, and is the current Duchess of Dellborough. She is the estranged aunt of Moriah Henshaw, and appears in THE TALONS OF LYON and TO CLAIM A LYON'S HEART.

Versey, Jenna – She is the wife of the eldest son and heir of Percy and Aurelia Versey, the Duke and Duchess of Dellborough. She appears in THE TALONS OF THE LYON.

Versey, Lancelot "Lance" – He's the hero of THE TALONS OF THE LYON, and is the younger brother of the Duke of Dellborough. He also appears in TO CLAIM A LYON'S HEART.

Versey, Percy – He is the older brother of Lance Versey, and is the current Duke of Dellborough. He appears in THE TALONS OF THE LYON and TO CLAIM A LYON'S HEART.

Versey, Seraphina Frogmore – She's the heroine of THE TALONS OF THE LYON, and is the widow of the late Baron Frogmore. She also appears in TO CLAIM A LYON'S HEART.

Wade, _________ – Lady Wade is the mother of Lady Diana Wade. She appears in FED TO THE LYON.

Wade, Geoffrey – Lord Wade is the father of Lady Diana Wade. He appears in FED TO THE LYON.

Walcot, Bertram – He is a professor at Cambridge, and is the father of Charlotta "Lottie" Walcot Grey, through his affair with Mrs. Bessie Dove-Lyon. He appears in PRETTY LITTLE LYON.

Watson, ________ – He is a fellow physician and colleague of Dr. Duncan Neilson, and is based out Of England. He appears in THE LYON'S DEN IN WINTER.

Webb, Anna Toussaint – She is the heroine of LYON AT THE ALTAR, and was the daughter of Frank Webb's former French tutor.

Webb, Bertha – She is the widow of the late James Webb, and is the current dowager Viscountess De-Wold. She appears in LYON AT THE ALTAR.

Webb, Frank – He is the hero of LYON AT THE ALTAR, and is the current Viscount De-Wold.

Webb, James – He is the late husband of Bertha Webb, and was the previous Viscount De-Wold before his passing. He appears in LYON AT THE ALTAR.

Wilson, ________ – He is the Marquess of Huntsford, and is the father of Stephanie and Eloise Wilson. He appears in THE COUR-AGE OF A LYON.

Wilson, Marguerite – She is the Marchioness of Huntsford, and is the mother of Stephanie and Eloise Wilson. She appears in THE COURAGE OF A LYON.

Wilson, Stephanie – She is the eldest daughter of the Marquess and Marchioness of Huntsford, and the eldest sister to Eloise Wilson. She appears in THE COURAGE OF A LYON.

Winwood, ________ – Lady Costerbridge is the mother of Juliet Winwood, and appears in LYON EYES.

Winwood, ________ – Lord Costerbridge is the father of Juliet Winwood, and appears in LYON EYES.

Winwood, Juliet – She is the daughter of Lord and Lady Costerbridge, and is the potential match for Miles, Duke of Goldthorpe. She appears in LYON EYES.

Witt, Mortimer – He is a business associate of Mr. Forest Prescott, and appears in THE LYON'S LAIRD.

Wolf, Adriana Benton – Heroine of THE LYON'S SHARE. She was first married to Baron Paul Benton, and after his passing she married Sidney Wolf.

Wolf, Sidney – Hero of THE LYON'S SHARE, and 6th Earl of Middlethorpe. He was the childhood friend of both Paul and Adriana Benton.

Wortham, Coraline Keyes – She is the younger sister of Madeline Keyes, and married Edmund Wortham, her sister's former betrothed. She appears in TAMED BY THE LYON.

Wortham, Edmund – He was formerly betrothed to Madeline Keyes, but married her younger sister, Coraline Keyes. He appears in TAMED BY THE LYON.

Worthington, Evelyn – She is the pious aunt of Lord Barker, and appears in THE TALONS OF THE LYON. She also appears in TO CLAIM A LYON'S HEART.

Wren, _______ – Mr. Wren is a Bow Street Runner, hired to solve the attempted murder of the Duke of Kendall. He appears in THE HEART OF A LYON.

_______, Bess – She is a pre-teen orphan, sent to live with Josiah and Amelia Barrymore by Mrs. Dove-Lyon. She appears in THE LYON'S SECRET.

_______, Daniel – Lord Daniel is the hero of LYON HEARTED, and is the second son of the Earl of Walden. He is also an art collector and seller, and is close friends with Prinny.

_______, Davina – She is the former childhood friend and possible wife for Cheyne Lyon when they were younger. She later married a Duke and became known as Duchess Davina. She appears in THE LYON'S SURPRISE.

_______, Everett – He is a former associate of Malcolm Black, and had paid Mr. Barney to kidnap Viola Black. He appears in THE LYON'S DEN IN WINTER.

__________, Garahan – He is one of the Duke of Wyndmere's guards, and appears in RESCUED BY THE LYON.

__________, Gerard – He is the Duke of Hillcrest, and is the best friend of Frank Webb, Viscount De-Wold. He appears in LYON AT THE ALTAR.

__________, Isolde – She is the younger sister of Percy and Lance Versey, and is a married countess. She appears in THE TALONS OF THE LYON.

__________, Joseph – He is the youngest son of Nessie and the late Lord Peder. He appears in LYON HEARTED.

__________, Kitty – She is the young niece of Peter Dermott, and appears in HOW TO STEAL A LYON'S FORTUNE.

__________, Li-Na – She is the heroine of LYON HEARTED, and marries Lord Daniel. She was also known as the Abacus Woman in the Lyon's Den. She is from China, and Mrs. Bessie Dove-Lyon won her freedom from a ship captain in a card game.

__________, Lucius – He is a friend of Vincent St. John, and is the Earl of Blackthorn. He appears in TO CLAIM A LYON'S HEART.

__________, Nessie – She is the dowager Countess of Walden, wife to the late Lord Peder, and mother to Stefan and Joseph. She appears in LYON HEARTED.

__________, Nineve – She is the younger sister of Percy and Lance Versey, and is married to a commoner, who is in service to the government. She appears in THE TALONS OF A LYON.

__________, Prinny – The Prince Regent appears in LYON HEART-ED, and is a close friend of Lord Daniel. He purchases artwork from him.

__________, Roger – He's the Earl of Harrowby, and is the estranged grandfather of Moriah Henshaw. He appears in TO CLAIM A LYON'S HEART.

___________, Stefan – He is the current Earl of Walden, and is the young nephew of Lord Daniel. He appears in LYON HEARTED.

___________________ – She's the Duchess of Winshire, and was previously the Duchess of Haverford. After her late husband, the Duke of Haverford, passed away, she married the Duke of Winshire. She's the mother of the current Duke of Haverford. She appears in TO CLAIM A LYON'S HEART.

___________________ – He's the current Duke of Haverford. His mother is the current Duchess of Winshire. His father is the late Duke of Haverford. He appears in TO CLAIM A LYON'S HEART.

Bessie Dove-Lyons & Employee Characters in The Lyon's Den

This is a list of all employee characters from the Lyon's Den novels.
A reference guide only.
All Characters are copyrighted.

Bessie Dove-Lyon – She is the mysterious widow of Colonel Sandstrom T. Lyon, who was rumored to be a much older man. She is also known as the Black Widow of Whitehall, and is the owner of the Lyon's Den. In THE LYON'S LADY LOVE it is revealed she has an older and estranged sister named Florence Blackwell. Their parents were criminals. Bessie had killed her father and ran away from the crime scene. In HOW TO STEAL A LYON'S FORTUNE, her late husband's nephew, Vincent Lyon, is in possession of a nude painting of her when she was a courtesan. She also removes her veil when speaking of family matters with Audrey Ruston (former stepdaughter of her nephew, Vincent Lyon). She is present in every novel in this series and is usually heavily veiled in black from head to toe. In PRETTY LITTLE LYON it is revealed that she is the birth mother of Charlotta "Lottie" Walcot. She sets up her daughter with her childhood love interest, Septimus Grey, who is also an investigator for Mrs. Dove-Lyon. Charlotta's father had an affair with Mrs. Dove Lyon when she was a courtesan. In THE LYON'S SECRET, her childhood friend, Mrs. Fielding, is the mother of Amelia Fielding.

Daniel Bates – He is a doorman at the Lyon's Den and appears in PRETTY LITTLE LYON.

Demetrius – He is a bouncer at the Lyon's Den, and appears in THE LYON'S LADY LOVE and PRIDE OF LYONS.

Egeus – He is a servant at the Lyon's Den, and appears in FED TO THE LYON, THE LYON'S LADY LOVE, LOVED BY THE LYON, THE COURAGE OF A LYON, and LYON AT THE ALTAR.

Joseph – He is the new jewelry apprentice to Mr. Gold in the Dragon's Hoard. He appears in INTO THE LYON'S DEN.

Helena – She is a servant in the Lyon's Den, and appears in THE LYON'S PUZZLE, LYON AT THE ALTAR, CAPTIVATED BY THE LYON, and TO CLAIM A LYON'S HEART.

Helene – She's also known as Mrs. Crutch. She is a go-between for her employer, Mrs. Dove-Lyon and appears in THE HEART OF A LYONINTO THE LYON OF FIRE.

Heleus – He is in charge of the attendants in the Lyon's Den. He appears in THE LYON SLEEPS TONIGHT.

Hermia – She is a wolf at the Lyon's Den, and appears in THE LYON'S LADY LOVE, ALWAYS THE LYON TAMER, A LYON'S PRIDE, LYON OF THE HIGHLANDS, LYON AT THE ALTAR, CAPTIVATED BY THE LYON, THE LYON AND THE LAMB, and TO CLAIM A LYON'S HEART.

Hippolyta – She is the pit boss in the Lyon's Den, and appears in INTO THE LYON'S DEN and THE LYON'S LADY LOVE.

Li-Na – She is the heroine of LYON HEARTED, and is also known as the Abacus Woman in INTO THE LYON'S DEN. She occupies a space next to the Gohar (Gold) family in their jewelry store in the Lyon's Den.

Lysander – He is an escort at the door of the Lyon's Den, and appears in FED TO THE LYON and THE LYON'S LADY LOVE.

Mr. Vance – He's the high-ranking representative at the card tables in the Lyon's Den. He appears in THE LYON'S PUZZLE.

Oberon – She's a female card dealer in the Lyon's Den. She appears in TO CLAIM A LYON'S HEART.

Petrushka – She is a gilded acrobat performer in the Lyon's Den. She appears in THE LYON AND THE LAMB.

Philostrate – He is a mute guardian at the Lyon's Den, and appears in INTO THE LYON'S DEN, THE LYON'S LADY LOVE, and THE HEART OF A LYON.

Puck – He is a bouncer at the Lyon's Den, and appears in THE LYON'S LADY LOVE and TO CLAIM A LYON'S HEART.

Pyramus – He is a bouncer at the Lyon's Den and appears in LYON EYES.

Snug – He is one of the wolf escorts at the Lyon's Den, and appears in RESCUED BY THE LYON, CAPTIVATED BY THE LYON, and TO CLAIM A LYON'S HEART.

Themisto – She is a servant at the Lyon's Den and appears in THE LYON SLEEPS TONIGHT.

Theseus – He is a wolf at the entrance at The Lyon's Den, and appears in THE LYON'S LADY LOVE, LOVED BY THE LYON, and LYON AT THE ALTAR.

Titan (AKA Luke Cross) – He is the future Earl of Wolvesmead, and is the head of the Wolf Pack of bouncers in the Lyon's Den. He is also known as Lord Lucifer. In RESCUED BY THE LYON he has a maimed hand from his war service. He appears in INTO THE LYON'S DEN, FED TO THE LYON, LYON'S PREY, PRETTY LITTLE LYON, THE COURAGE OF A LYON, LYON AT THE ALTAR, CAPTIVATED BY THE LYON, and THE LYON AND THE LAMB.

Notes

In case you'd like to add your own notes until the next update….

And More Notes

And More Notes

And More Notes

And More Notes

In conclusion...

As I've said, this guide will be updated as necessary because more books will be added to the Lyon's Den Connected World.

Until then, please enjoy using this guide while reading.